TEJASWY NANDURY manages a proprietary fund that trades currencies, equities, commodities and fixed income. Managing funds for over a decade across various asset instruments classes has given him a unique perspective into the operation of global capital markets. Prior to being a fund manager, he worked in the field of private equity where he was exposed to a broad range of businesses in critical growth phases.

Nandury began his career as a Management Consultant at McKinsey & Co. where he worked primarily in the fields of telecom and technology. As a student, he worked at the World Bank in the Development Economics Vice Presidency under Nobel Laureate Joseph Stiglitz where he explored the relationship between the openness of economies and their GDP growth rates.

Tejaswy Nandury holds a bachelor's degree in Economics from Stanford University. Presently, he lives in Mumbai with his wife.

Multi-baggers

Investing in MEGA RETURN STOCKS

Tejaswy Nandury

www.visionbooksindia.com

www.visionbooksindia.com

Disclaimer

The author and the publisher disclaim all legal or other responsibilities for any losses which investors may suffer by investing or trading using the methods described in this book. Readers are advised to seek professional guidance before making any specific investments. This book is meant purely for the purpose of investor and trader education.

First Published 2011
Reprinted 2013, 2015, 2016, 2017, 2019, 2020, 2021, 2022, 2023, 2024

ISBN 10: 81-7094-837-1
ISBN 13: 978-81-7094-837-7

Published by
Vision Books Pvt. Ltd.
(Incorporating Orient Paperbacks and CARING imprints)
24 Feroze Gandhi Road, Lajpat Nagar 3
New Delhi-110024, India.
Phone: (+91-11) 2984 0821 / 22
e-mail: visionbooks@gmail.com

Printed at
Saurabh Printers
67A-68, Ecotech 1, Extn 1, Kasna, Greater Noida
Uttar Pradesh, India.

Contents

PART - 2

Some Indian Multibagger Examples

Preface

I began writing this book in March 2008, in the middle of one of the most vicious bear markets ever seen in history. Stock market indices around the world collapsed in the following months. Every asset class froze and we saw the first credit panic in a very long time. Writing a book about multibaggers in that environment seemed, to be very charitable, foolhardy. At the same time, it also seemed unfair that my research team and I had built up such a wealth of knowledge on the subject over several years of being active investors. We also felt that the dramatic compression in value would create a fantastic investment environment when the market began to turn up. However, at no point during the writing of this book did it become obvious that we had broken out of a bear market into a bull market, or that the problems of the credit crisis will not come back to haunt us in another fashion soon. Yet, in one way, the time was ideal: our ideas could be tested in real time by readers of this book.

A key concept that I have tried to emphasize several times in this book is that investment is multi-disciplinary. One has to engage all of one's senses to be a consistently successful investor. This means that you need a little bit of many skills but not necessarily great depth of expertise in any one aspect of investment, such as fundamental analysis or technical analysis, macroeconomics or any sectoral specializations. This multi-disciplinary approach is especially essential in the pursuit of multibaggers because they come from the oddest and most unexpected of places. Investors need to be alert to changes in the real world, understand a bit of economics, finance, valuation, technical analysis, and have patience and conviction in their own ideas in order to be able to generate multibagger returns from stocks that appreciate dramatically.

I could not have completed this book without the assistance of my team: Sreedhar Babu Kanuri, Sharath Jutur and Gayathri Khandavalli. My publisher, Kapil Malhotra, offered several ideas that helped refine the book and was very active in encouraging me to write whenever I lost momentum. I also want to thank my father, who was kind enough to read an early draft and offer his comments, and my mother, who goaded me into finishing it. Lastly, I could not have written this without the understanding and support of Suchitra, my wife. Her patience with my constant obsession with financial markets helped me spend the time required to build a body of knowledge on the subject.

This work is by no means the definitive study on this subject. No investment book can be. But, hopefully, it highlights the key aspects that are necessary to identify, hold and sell multibaggers and I hope the framework will stand the test of time.

TEJASWY NANDURY

Hyderabad,
July 2011

PART

1

Multibaggers: An Introduction

By 2009, Infosys had appreciated by 25,000% since its public issue in 1993. Similarly, Dr. Reddy's Labs had returned over 600 times the original investment amount since 1993. Very few investors in the world can claim to have captured these types of eye-popping returns, which are every investor's dream. Such returns are commonly dismissed as being just a product of luck or of gambling. However, our research shows that multibaggers share several characteristics that can be identified by those willing to put in the work required. In this book, we have tried to distil the common characteristics of stocks that can generate such returns. Though we have spent a lot of time trying to understand the common characteristics of multibaggers, these common characteristics are neither necessary nor sufficient conditions for earning a multibagger return. Several companies will have the characteristics that are identified in this book but will never appreciate significantly. There will be other companies which have none of the characteristics that this book identifies but will still earn tremendous returns for their investors. While this may appear contradictory, one has to understand that business and investing are unpredictable fields where strange things happen on a very frequent basis.

What are Multibaggers?

For the purposes of this book, I am restricting the definition of multibagger to any stock that can generate a return of greater than 1,000%, i.e. a ten-fold return over a 5- to 10-year period. After a rigorous analysis of all the multibaggers that the Indian stock market has produced since 1990, we have identified common characteristics that stocks which produce these type of outstanding returns possess. Since investors can only take advantage of identifiable opportunities, one of the criteria that we used to narrow down our list was that an alert investor should be able to identify such opportunities. We did not consider companies with limited disclosures that made it impossible to identify them as possible multibaggers in our study.

It is also important to note that all companies that fit the criteria we have outlined will not become multibaggers. There are challenges in business execution, management capability, technological factors as well as new products, competition, etc., that will restrict some companies from being able to reach the levels that an investor might dream up for them. One of the key skills is to be able to get out of such situations without getting emotionally attached and stay with only those stocks that go on to become multibaggers.

Are All Good Companies Multibaggers?

In general discourse, people often refer to certain companies as good companies. There is also an implicit assumption that such companies will make good investments. We beg to differ. Good companies will become multibaggers only if they are bought at proper prices. Good companies can also generate losses for investors if investors buy their shares at the wrong time. So do not automatically assume that because you are buying a great company, you will get a multibagger return. However, if you are able to buy a great company at a time of high pessimism, you are more likely to generate a multibagger return over the long term.

> Good companies will become multibaggers only if they are bought at proper prices.

How to Generate Multibagger Returns

There are four parts to generating a multibagger return:

- Identifying a suitable company;
- Buying its stock at the right time;
- Holding the stock until the potential of the company is more than fully captured in its price, and
- Exiting.

Each of these four parts is very important. In contemporary stock market literature, a lot of attention is paid to identifying good companies but rarely ever are the other aspects of generating multibagger returns equally highlighted.

Identifying a Suitable Company

Let us first tackle the identification of the opportunity. You need to learn to identify potential multibaggers in industries experiencing growth. In Chapter 2, we will outline criteria for identifying potential multibaggers. Investors need to study these criteria carefully and understand them well in order to develop this skill.

Buying at the Right Time

Just because you have identified a potential multibagger company does not mean you should jump in and buy its stock. You need to understand whether you are buying it at the right price. How does one do that? There are a few circumstances in which a purchase decision increases the probability of generating a multibagger return. Let's consider what these are.

Buying a Company in a New Industry Early in its Lifecycle

You need to identify an industry that is either new or experiencing a positive change that will benefit companies in the industry. Then you need to find suitable investment candidate within the industry and buy its stock before there is widespread recognition of its potential. This would be akin to having bought Hero Honda or Zee Telefilms in 1993. Both were good companies in nascent industries and in 1993 their potential was not fully recognized. However, this approach is fraught with risk because the new industry may not grow as you envision. It is possible to de-risk this contingency by only buying those companies that are trading at a significant discount to their extrinsic valuation, a concept which is covered later in this book. Buying at a Price / Sales (P/S) ratio below 1 or a Price / Earnings (P/E) ratio below 10 in a new industry can also significantly protect the downside risk.

Buying a Good Company with Demonstrated Growth in a Market Panic

This involves look for a company with proven capability in a growing industry. For the purposes of this book, a market panic is a situation in which the market falls by more than 30%, and when market indices such as the Sensex or Nifty are trading at Price / Earnings ratios below 12. Typically, these market panics affect all companies, whether they are good or bad. Therefore, at such times, share prices even of good companies are beaten down to highly attractive, bargain basement levels. These market panics usually occur because of a need for liquidity and a fear psychosis among traders and investors rather than due to any fundamental problems with the companies themselves. Those who have identified suitable companies, as explained in Chapter 2, can apply the same valuations as in the first case, namely Price / Sales ratio below 1 or Price / Earnings ratio below 10, to purchase shares of those companies during a market panic. Though share prices may fall below your purchase prices for a while, buying good companies at attractive prices will generate good returns over the long run.

Buying a Company with Proven Capability Experiencing Temporary Problems in a Growth Sector

Even the best companies in the world cannot deliver outstanding results every quarter. Due to various market and execution related problems, good companies sometimes have bad quarters. Even if the management team of a company has demonstrated consistent ability to generate sales and profits in different market conditions, the market tends to punish the shares of such companies when they are experiencing a temporary problem. However, for the long term buyer this is a great purchase opportunity. The caveat, however, is that the problems should be of a temporary nature and the share price should fall sufficiently so that it is attractive enough to compensate you for the risk you are taking. Again, we apply the same ratios as earlier. Buy these companies if their shares are trading at Price / Sales ratios below 1 or their Price / Earnings ratios are below 10.

Holding a Multibagger for the Long Haul

The third aspect of generating multibagger returns is less a skill and more of an attitude. Holding for the long term is critical to generating multibagger returns. Markets have several ups and downs. Multibaggers tend to move far more sharply in either direction than the overall market. Several factors affect both the market and individual stocks. It is important to think of multibaggers as businesses and not as stocks. Those who let the price of their investments, or the movements of the index, affect their view of the underlying business will not be able to extract multibagger returns even if they can identify likely multibagger companies. In fact, the time taken to generate multibagger returns is usually at least five years. While holding multibaggers, investors will experience severe price volatility, self doubt, and pain. At the same time, there are occasional doubts whether the company's fundamental performance justifies being invested in it. Being able to answer this question and possessing patience are the only ways to getting multibagger returns.

Exiting a Multibagger

Identifying, buying and holding a multibagger are difficult, but the sell call is the most challenging. Sometimes stocks will look highly overpriced and it may appear worthwhile selling them.

We deal with this issue in greater depth in Chapter 4, but here is a brief introduction.

When the Company's Shares become Extrinsically Overvalued

We will deal with the concept of extrinsic valuation in greater depth in Chapter 2. Briefly, a high extrinsic valuation means that a company's market capitalization either approaches, or overshoots, the size of the external opportunity, i.e. the size of the industry or sector it is in. When the market is willing to be so aggressive about valuing a company, it is worth thinking about exiting. Rarely, if ever, is there a company that has 100% market share. If the stock market wishes to ascribe such a valuation to a company that you have invested in, you should oblige people who have this view and sell your shares to them.

When the Company's Shares Become Intrinsically Overvalued

If the market is willing to pay a Price / Sales (P/S) ratio of over 15 or Price / Earnings (P/E) ratio of over 50, it is worth thinking about selling the shares of that company. This does not mean that the shares will not go up. However, it does mean that the prices are unrealistic, don't have too much further upside, and are unlikely to sustain in the long run. There may be other opportunities that can generate better returns with greater safety. So it is best for one to book profits.

When Indices Become Overvalued

Sometimes market bubbles are created because the consensus opinion in the market becomes very optimistic. The overvaluation of indices become obvious through the index P/E. If the Sensex or Nifty begins to trade at P/E ratios of over 25, as it did in 1992, in 2000, and again in 2008, then it is time to sell all your holdings to the optimists and wait for some pessimism to set in for making purchases.

When Alternate Opportunities Look Like Multibaggers

The question of whether to hold or sell should also be guided by alternate opportunities which can generate a superior return. If exiting your present holding and buying another stock will generate better returns, it is worth doing so.

When a Company or Industry Fails to Deliver

Sometimes, what looked like a good opportunity may not turn out to be so. In such a case, there is no point in hanging on to a company that has consistently failed to increase sales. It is best to sell such companies and move on to others.

Multibaggers are not for everybody. While some exposure to potential multibaggers can add return to the average portfolio, investors also need to understand their own personal cash flows and their tolerance of volatility to capture these returns. Multibagger opportunities are ideally suited for those people who do not have to worry about using the cash that they have invested in such companies for a considerable length of time. Those who need this cash will be prone to worrying about volatility and will have a very difficult time generating multibagger returns.

Also, at this point it is worth talking a little bit about leverage. For most investors, borrowing money to invest in stocks is a bad idea. The Indian market is especially volatile and companies that tend to become multibaggers are more volatile than others. Borrowing money makes it impossible to hold stocks of such companies for the long term and adds an element of unnecessary risk. Remember, leverage is typically not for investors, it is for traders.

This book covers all these issues and then goes on to use recent Indian multibaggers as examples to illustrate the concepts that are outlined. In our experience, multibaggers are generated through a combination of alertness, diligence, patience and willingness to think independently. These are soft issues that we have identified which an investor will only learn over a period of time. We have attempted to provide a framework for the harder skills required but it is up to you to develop these soft skills and attitudes in order to succeed in your quest for multibaggers.

At first glance, this book might make it seem that there is some formula to generating high returns. In fact, the central message of the book is that there is no formula. We are only generalizing from specific examples of multibaggers that we have already seen. So while you read this book, keep in mind that investing is not formulaic. In fact, it is an art that takes a lifetime to get good at. Every investment rule has at least two exceptions, which is why experience and a multi-disciplinary approach are absolutely essential for multibagger investment success. We are only attempting to provide a few concepts that can form the basis of a multi-disciplinary approach towards generating multibagger returns. Good luck and happy investing.

2

Identifying Multibaggers

The first, and probably the easiest, step in earning multibagger returns is to identify stocks that have the potential to generate extraordinary returns. In order to understand what makes a multibagger, we researched stocks that appreciated more than 1,000% in the Indian market in rolling 5-year periods from 1990 to 2008. Using this data as a starting point, we distilled out the characteristics that were common to all multibaggers. In addition to this, we looked at several international multibaggers and tried to identify what made them so. These international multibaggers give us some clues as to the direction that India could take in the future. But one needs to be cautious and not extrapolate too much since India is charting its own unique course due to its inherent opportunities and constraints.

One key qualitative criterion we used was that at the time of purchase, the potential for having multibagger returns had to be *identifiable.* The reason for highlighting the identifiable multibagger potential at the time of purchase is that the world of global finance is so dynamic that the unexpected occurs regularly. Almost no one can predict how exactly the world will change. Due to this reason, multibaggers that are totally unexpected and inexplicable are regular features of great bull markets. Our requirement that potential had to be identifiable weeded out stocks like Jai Corp, Marathon Nextgen Realty or BF Utilities which, in the 2003-2008 period, generated tremendous returns (59,900%, 5,84,718%, and 37,847%, respectively). While some of these stocks could have been value picks in 2003, it was very difficult for an investor who was not an insider to either get information about these companies or identify them as having any multibagger potential in 2003 (or in 2008, for that matter!).

Good Companies *versus* Multibaggers

A common misconception among many market participants is that good companies will generate multibagger returns. That is not the case. Good companies, at best, guarantee protection of principal over the long term. In the short term, good companies can sometimes generate even very negative returns. Good companies that are bought at the wrong price will not generate multibagger returns. A great example is Infosys. Infosys is a very good company. But an investor who purchased its stock in 2000 would not have earned his principal back until 2006. Good companies have to be bought when the price that they are selling at ignores or significantly understates their market potential.

> Good companies have to be bought when the price that they are selling at ignores or significantly understates their market potential.

The Lifecycle of a Multibagger

From our study we identified that a multibagger goes through several phases, as conceptualized in Figure 2.1. In the first phase, most multibagger stocks experience an improvement in fundamentals but the market does not recognize this improvement. This lack of market recognition is manifested in low trading volumes, low institutional interest in the stock, low analyst coverage and extremely low valuations. In this phase, the entire market capitalization of the company is usually below ₹500 crore. The stock typically trades in a very narrow range and is likely to experience one or two sharp corrections. In this first phase, you can buy the stock at any point to generate high returns and much attention need not be paid on timing a purchase so long as the criteria outlined later in this chapter are met.

In Phase II, there is greater awareness in the market about the company's improving performance and prospects. The company moves from being a small cap to a mid-cap and at some point in this phase will probably see a market capitalization of greater than ₹1,000 crore. Brokers will initiate coverage in the company, volumes pick up, and institutional interest also gets generated. Valuations become reasonable but not excessive. This second phase also usually ends with a large correction after a significant run-up in the stock price, which brings valuations back into attractive territory. In Phase II, it is best to buy after sharp corrections because a badly timed purchase in this phase will reduce overall return.

In the third phase, recognition levels are very high and the stock price starts a vertical climb. The stock will move up on every bit of good news and will appreciate dramatically in a very short

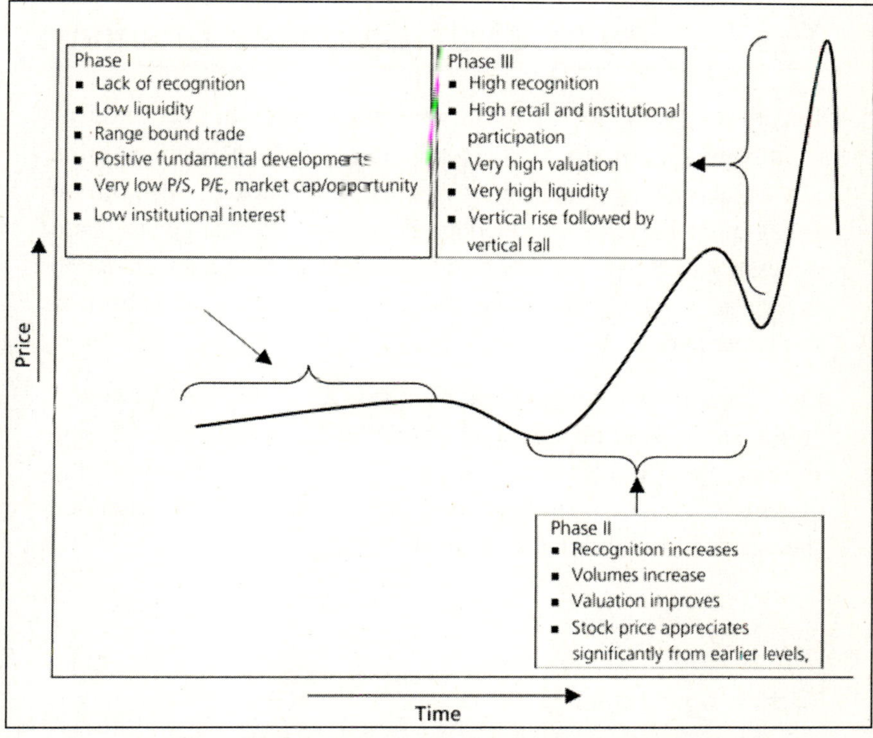

Figure 2.1: **Different phases in the lifecycle of a multibagger**

---

time. Valuations become highly stretched but people continue buying the stock regardless. Both institutional and retail interest becomes very high. From this point on, the stock will only generate moderate returns even if it is held for the long term. This is the time to be selling the stock to all the eager late-comers who want to buy. Even though there may be temptation to buy, purchases should be avoided at all costs.

The Framework of Unrecognized Change

Let us now shift to the thesis that emerged from our study of multibaggers, namely that finding unrecognized change is the key to achieving multibagger returns. Both lack of recognition — as manifested in low valuations — and the change itself are necessary in order to generate high investment returns. Once the market as a whole recognizes the change, returns can at best be moderate and, at worst, negative.

One often hears the cliché that change is the only constant factor. In the case of multibaggers, change is the critical factor. Change creates opportunities that did not exist earlier and alters the course of various businesses and industries. So, let us examine the various kinds of change that can occur.

Types of Change

Technological Change

This is a very simple concept. A new technology replaces an old technology. Cars replaced horse carriages, emails replaced snail mail, compact discs replaced cassette tapes, and cell phones replaced landlines. The list is endless. Technological change is quite obvious and visible to most people. However, most people don't immediately correlate the change to stock market gains and take advantage of it. Sometimes the opportunity due to a technology change is created not just in the technology provider but also in the user of such a technology.

Macro Change

By a macro change, we mean a change that occurs in an industry, or a country, as a whole that can positively (or negatively) influence the value of certain stocks. This change can manifest itself either as a societal, demographic or economic trend. Examples of such changes are the secular uptrend in crude oil prices that began in 1999, the global reduction of interest rates following the 9/11 attacks, or the shift among Indian consumers from scooters to motorcycles. Such circumstantial changes become visible only over a period of time but one of the keys to finding multibaggers is to catch such changes early on.

Company-Specific Change

Sometimes, change occurs within a company. Either the ownership or management changes, or the company gets restructured, or there is a merger or acquisition that changes the course that a company takes. These types of changes can also generate dramatic returns if caught early enough. The same company under a different management can often produce very high returns. This is a phenomenon that is more obvious in international markets than in India. But in the future, in India too we are likely to see more and more management buy outs (MBOs), leveraged buy outs (LBOs) and mergers and acquisitions, which place existing companies in the hands of new managements.

Identifying Change

Here, it is worth spending some time understanding how one can notice change.

Sometimes, it is very obvious. In the early 1990s, you would have noticed that urban Indians stopped watching Doordarshan and started watching Zee TV. Or in the early part of the first decade of the 21st century, you would have noticed that everyone was buying mobile phones. If you were financially oriented, you would have noticed that the price of crude started rising from 2000 onwards. Alert individuals can always perceive change just by observing the world around them. Translating this observation into an investment idea is slightly more involved and only the most motivated people tend to do this.

Lack of Recognition of Change

The second aspect of the concept of unrecognized change that needs to be understood is the lack of recognition. This lack of market recognition manifests itself in a few ways.

Low Extrinsic Valuations

You would have often heard of the intrinsic value of a company. Here, I present a new concept, namely extrinsic value. I define extrinsic value as the value of a company in relation to the total size of the external opportunity, i.e. the market. This crystallizes itself in the ratio of market capitalization of the company to the opportunity size. So a low extrinsic valuation means a low market capitalization to external opportunity ratio. To illustrate, let us take the example of Hero Honda in 1993. The stock traded at a market capitalization of about ₹200 crore when a conservative estimate of the size of its potential opportunity was ₹20,000 crore. Unitech, in 2001, had a market capitalization of ₹56 crore whereas its addressable market opportunity was probably as large as ₹10,00,000 crore. Such low market capitalization in relation to the addressable opportunity is a clear sign of the market ignoring a company's potential. Make no mistake: the calculation of an addressable opportunity is highly subjective. The trick is to make a very conservative estimate of market opportunity and buy a good company that is trading at greater than 80% discount to this conservative calculation. That means you are looking to buy companies that have a market capitalization to opportunity ratio of less than 0.2. Granted, this is not scientific, but no valuation metric that is presently used by the priests of high finance is scientific.

Low Traditional Valuation Ratios

While extrinsic valuation is at the core of this book, intrinsic value, as reflected in traditional valuation ratios is also important. Though traditional valuation ratios such as Price / Earnings (P/E) ratios and Price / Book Value (P/B) ratios can sometimes be very misleading, typically low ratios are a sign that the market does not place a very high premium on the companies concerned. An investor who understands that a change is taking place in a certain industry should be willing to take cues from very low valuation ratios. P/E ratios below 10 and P/B ratios below 1 can be considered very low. For example, Unitech sold at a P/E of about 8 in 2002. It is important to remember that even though I am suggesting these metrics, I would like to stress that valuation is only one of the many tools that one should employ when evaluating potential multibaggers. Multibaggers tend to defy straight-line logic. A formulaic approach will hardly help you identify or invest in multibaggers and valuations are nothing but formulae. Do not rely solely on traditional valuations. Neither should you completely ignore valuations. Valuations can help you avoid making big mistakes.

Low Price / Sales Ratio

Several potential multibaggers have very low earnings or may even be incurring losses at the time that they are attractive purchase opportunities. The traditional P/E ratio, which a lot of people focus on, makes no sense in these cases. In such situations, the price to sales ratio can be a great sanity check. Generally, a P/S value of less than 1 can be considered very attractive. Let me reiterate the reason for this: a multibagger return can only be captured by entering a stock when it is early in its cycle. At such an early stage in its cycle, the company is likely to be financially feeble. It will generate anaemic profits. These profits will grow tremendously if you have identified the right company. But they will not be apparent on the day you want to invest. When there are no profits, the P/E ratio is either likely to be negative or absurdly high. So the P/E ratio will look unattractive at a time when the stock is actually very attractive. Which is why it is better to look for another sanity check, that is, the P/S ratio. A company that is not trading at a Price / Sales ratio of even 1 is very cheap even if its P/E ratio is very high.

A company that is not trading at a Price / Sales ratio of even 1 is very cheap even if its P/E ratio is very high.

So I tend to look for an attractive price through the P/S ratio when the P/E ratio is very high in a stock that meets the other criteria described here. Do keep in mind that some industries with very low margins have low P/S ratios. Industries of this type include trading, commodity-oriented businesses and some financial businesses. So an investment in a business with great prospects and a very high P/E ratio can sometimes, but not always, be justified by a low P/S ratio.

Lack of Liquidity

Stocks that are highly liquid are those which have plenty of investor interest. Very low liquidity typically implies that the market at large has not yet recognized the potential of a certain stock and is not trading in it very aggressively. This presents a great opportunity for shrewd investors to accumulate a stock with great potential when there is poor liquidity and sell the stock when liquidity kicks in at a later date. For instance, the stock of Welspun Gujarat Stahl Rohren had a 365-day average traded turnover of ₹10 lakh in 2001. By the end of 2007, when the stock was well recognized, the 365-day average traded turnover jumped to ₹24 crore. Between 2001 and 2007 the stock appreciated 47 times. If you had invested in the same stock in, say, 2006 when it was well recognized, it would have appreciated by 3 times. That is not a terrible return, but it is no multibagger. However, remember that if you need money in the short term, buying an illiquid stock can be disastrous. Never attempt to do multibagger investing with money that you may need in the next couple of years. Multibaggers are only for those who have a long term horizon and reasonable financial independence.

Absence of Institutional Investors

Indian investors are wont to look for foreign institutional investor (FII) or mutual fund holdings in a stock in order to gain confidence that their judgment is correct. However, one of the key signals of a lack of recognition is the lack of institutional holdings in the stock. Typically, institutions do not like to enter illiquid stocks because they will not be able to sell them very quickly should they need to meet redemptions. By the time a stock becomes very liquid, in most cases the opportunity to make extraordinary returns is long gone. This is a key point to remember. Most institutions like liquidity because they have very large funds to invest and it is impossible for them to buy a stock that trades in very low volumes. Also, they may face redemption pressures from time to time. This forces them to only buy liquid stocks. However, by the time stocks become highly liquid, they are more likely to mimic index returns rather than generate multibagger returns. So, if you have identified a good company, then don't let the absence of institutional investors deter you. In fact, take encouragement that you have found a good company before others have discovered it.

Now that we have introduced the central concept of unrecognized change, it is time to look at a few other characteristics that we need to identify potential multibaggers.

Short-cuts to Unrecognized Change

It is now useful to combine lack of recognition and change. Unrecognized change can be identified using a short-cut: look for very low valuations. Our definition of lack of recognition is that the company's potential is not reflected in its market capitalization. This essentially means that the company should have a low extrinsic valuation as well as potentially low P/E and P/S ratios. Such companies are easily found by looking at the following situations.

Ignored Sectors

One of the easiest ways of identifying potential multibaggers is to look for sectors that the market is ignoring. On the other hand, just because the stock market is ignoring a sector does not mean that there are multibaggers to be found in that sector. But when a market ignores a sector, companies in that sector tend to trade at very low valuations. The key skill one has to develop to catch a multibagger is to be able to perceive positive change in an ignored sector and then take exposure to that sector in spite of bad news around it. A great example of such an ignored sector was real estate in 2002. Even though it was obvious that a very benign environment had been created for real estate, in 2002 the market did not yet care about this sector at all. An investor in Unitech would have reaped rich rewards.

The key skill one has to develop to catch a multibagger is to be able to perceive positive change in an ignored sector

Another such example was oil services. Companies like Aban Offshore traded at abysmal valuations after the crash of 2000 even though oil prices had started rising.

Infrastructure was also an example of such an out-of-favour sector. For the most part of their existence, infrastructure companies suffered from very low valuations compared to their potential. But, by 2001, it became obvious that the government was taking proactive steps to improve the country's infrastructure. However, for a while these companies traded at abysmal valuations.

New Sectors

Sometimes, new sectors come to the fore. The definition of a new sector is moot. However, typically, these are emerging sectors which are full of promise with very few listed companies. These companies tend to exhibit very high sales growth without commensurate bottom-line growth. The common perception in the market will be that it is a very high risk sector. Technical analysts will be highly bullish, though, thanks to the sector's momentum but value investors will be very wary of entering such companies because valuations would tend to be extremely stretched. However, for those willing to make a leap of faith, rewards can be substantial. Examples of such new sectors include organized retail in 2000, educational software, which came to the fore with the listing of Educomp Solutions, and motorcycles, which was a new sector in the 1990s. Such new sectors are risky bets but after a couple of years, the trend becomes very obvious. The right time to buy new sectors is when a trend in the real world is very obvious but the market, due to other factors, ignores this real world trend. Buying new sectors at such times can be very profitable in the long run.

> The right time to buy new sectors is when a trend in the real world is very obvious but the market ignores this real world trend.

Consider the example of Zee Telefilms. In 1993, satellite television was a new sector and Zee was the only listed company in this sector. Despite its aggressive growth, Zee's share price remained subdued for about four years. But in 1999 its stock price exploded and returned 10x in just one year. Someone who bought Zee early on in 1993 would have made a return of 150 times his original investment in the 2000 boom.

Beaten Down Good Companies in Market Downtrends

Sometimes market downtrends occur only because of liquidity reasons. This means that investors who need to raise cash urgently sell their positions in order to generate liquidity. There is no fundamental deterioration in the condition of the companies that people want to get out of. Such urgent demands for cash are created because the financial world is full of investors who borrow money to invest in stocks. Due to a reduction in available liquidity, these leveraged investors sometimes have to pay back the money that they have borrowed in a hurry. This results in meltdowns that have no apparent reason. In fact, a lot of recent market crashes have happened because of the model of "risk management" that a lot of leveraged investors follow. The 1987 world-wide market crash, the 1997 Asian crisis related world-wide equity downturn, and the May 2006 world-wide crash are examples of selling that was not based on fundamentals. Such liquidity-based crashes result in stock prices being bid down to absurdly low levels. At

> Liquidity-based crashes result in stock prices being bid down to absurdly low levels. At such times, buying good companies results in extraordinary investment returns.

such times, buying good companies results in extraordinary investment returns. However, buying when the share price is falling will more than likely lead to a loss of confidence. The best time to buy a company whose share price has fallen dramatically is to look for the price damage to cease. This means that the stock stops going down but it hasn't started going up yet. Generally, such a company will bounce back sharply if the broader market recovers.

Identifying Good Companies

A good company is one that is focused on a promising, expanding sector and has a good management team that can exploit opportunities. The greatest market opportunity in the world will turn to dust in the hands of teams that cannot execute. An investor may feel completely betrayed if he or she invests in the wrong company in the right sector. Execution capability is not obvious from day one. But if you find that a company is able to grow its sales and earnings with some consistency, you can be sure that they know how to execute.

If you find that a company is able to grow its sales and earnings with some consistency, you can be sure that they know how to execute.

What are the signs that one should look for in identifying good companies?

Large Market Potential

Multibaggers are very rarely created in niche industries. Niche industries may be highly specialized and exciting to those involved in them, but a company needs to achieve scale in order to deliver multibagger returns. Scale cannot be achieved in small niches. So, it is better to look at companies that are targeting a large number of customers or large value orders rather than those that focus on a small number of customers with small value orders. However, one caveat is necessary at this point. It is important to understand that though the company's target market needs to be potentially large, at the time of investment it may be relatively small. An example is Bharti Airtel. In the 1990s, cell phones were considered niche products aimed at rich business people who wanted to be in touch with others while on the move. A calculation of the market size then may have shown a very small number. In fact, in a now infamous gaffe, in the 1980s McKinsey & Co. advised AT&T not to enter the cell phone market because it was too small! The key insight to investing in Bharti when it listed was that communication was actually a mass need that went underserved in India, thanks to the public sector monopolies that then existed. In order to have invested in Bharti, it was essential to think of it as a communication service provider rather than as a rich peoples' status symbol service provider. It was also essential to understand that incremental telecommunications market share in India would go to the private sector rather than the public sector. Bharti was not just providing rich people with toys but was delivering an essential service with the efficiency of a private sector player. Having

It is important to understand that though the company's target market needs to be potentially large, at the time of investment it may be relatively small.

an expensive cell phone was vastly preferable to not having a phone at all or having a BSNL / MTNL landline. Only those who had this insight could have invested in Bharti at that time.

Good Sales Growth

Sales growth is a good reflection of the ability of a company to exploit opportunities. In fact, in a sense it is more relevant than profit growth because profits are difficult to accurately measure whereas sales are harder to fudge. So, look for high sales growth to identify good execution. Consider the case of Infosys. To start with, it was one among the very few players in the IT services sector. Between 1992 and 2000, sales grew tremendously from ₹9.38 crore to ₹884.35 crore. In order to become multibaggers, companies with total sales size of between ₹100 and ₹500 crore should have sales growth in the range of 50% per annum. Companies that have sales between ₹500 and ₹2,000 crore should have sales growth of at least 30% per annum. Companies that have sales above ₹2,000 crore should demonstrate sales growth of at least 20% per annum in order to be considered potential multibaggers.

Leadership in the Industry

Our study of multibaggers shows that the odds of success are better when one invests in a market leader, that is, the company with the largest market share. Typically, the fact that a company is a market leader in a certain sector implies the company is an early mover with execution capability. The fact that it has executed well and captured market share also indicates that it has some financial strength — though it is always better to verify this by studying the balance sheet. It can also sometimes indicate that the company has found a way to satisfy its customers better than its competition.

An example of this is Pantaloon Retail. Pantaloon was probably the earliest listed retail player in the country. Even though it had not done big box format stores like Big Bazaar earlier, it had garnered experience through its chain of garment stores. Once it set up Big Bazaar in Mumbai, it quickly executed this strategy and replicated its success in various other cities. It expanded faster than all the other retail chains and captured bigger retail market share than either Shoppers' Stop or Trent. It also delivered the best returns to investors from among this troika. It is, however, important to distinguish between market leaders and the first mover. The first mover may not be the market leader. The market leader is always the one with the largest market share. Generally, those without execution capability do not become market leaders.

It is, however, important to distinguish between market leaders and the first mover. The first mover may not be the market leader. The market leader is always the one with the largest market share.

Companies that Focus on New Initiatives

Companies that do not continuously innovate eventually become irrelevant and decline. Good companies are constantly innovating with new products, trying to penetrate new geographies, or entering new product segments. A company that does not develop new initiatives is not investing in its future. Therefore, such companies are not suited to long term investment.

Companies with Ability to Change Business Models to Suit Market Conditions

The world of business is ever-changing and dynamic. Companies that become successful are able to understand that the world is changing and react to those changes quickly and effectively. Companies that cannot react to change usually end up facing declining sales and profits.

An example of a company that has changed its business model several times to suit market conditions is Titan Industries. Titan was originally a watchmaker and a manufacturer of precision tools. Though Titan was always the trendier alternative to HMT, its watches were relatively staid by today's standards. As the market evolved, Titan acted dynamically to take advantage of evolving trends. Expecting branded jewellery to be a big segment, Titan rapidly expanded into this area through its Tanishq stores. Though Tanishq was a middling success, Titan also greatly enhanced its design capabilities in its watches division and introduced a slew of models and brands at various price points. Very quickly, Titan became the first choice for anyone wishing to buy a watch in India. This dynamism is easy to recognize *post-facto* but extremely difficult to anticipate. However, this is the one of the most important factors that will determine the returns a company can produce.

Companies with Good Reputation in the Industry

It is always worthwhile to talk to people in the industry to understand a company's standing. Philip Fisher, the great growth investor, promoted the concept of scuttlebutt. Scuttlebutt involves gaining as much information as possible about the prospective company from industry players and other stakeholders of the company by posing intelligent questions. Explaining scuttle-butt,

Fisher in his book *Common Stocks and Uncommon Profits and Other Writings* writes, "It is surprising what the scuttle method will produce. Until the average investor tries it, he probably will not believe how complete a picture will emerge if he asks intelligent questions about a company's research activities of a diversified group of research people, some from within the company and others engaged in related lines in competitive industries, in universities and in government."*

The Right Time to Buy Multibaggers

Remember, buying good companies at any price will not result in multibaggers. Buying good companies that have significantly low extrinsic valuations is what generates very high returns. There may be times where you have identified good companies but you will have to wait until they are available at very low prices in order to purchase them.

This begs the question of when it is appropriate to buy good companies. Timing the stock market is very difficult. But valuation can be a great sanity check. In addition to valuations, a good timing device is to wait for substantial falls in the market indices followed by periods of relative calm. If one were to adopt a rule based approach to time the market, there are three situations in which one should buy.

* *Common Stocks and Uncommon Profits and Other Writings,* Philip A. Fisher, Wiley Investment Classics.

Buying a Good Company in a New Industry Early in its Lifecycle

This means that you need to identify an industry that is either new or one which is experiencing a positive change which will benefit companies involved in the industry. Then you need to find a good company in that industry and buy its stock before there is widespread recognition of its potential. This would be akin to having bought Hero Honda or Zee Telefilms in 1993. Both were good companies in nascent industries and, in 1993, their potential was not widely recognized.

This approach is, however, fraught with risk because the new industry may not grow as you envision it. The good news is that it is possible to de-risk this by only buying companies that are trading at a significant discount to their extrinsic valuation, a concept which is covered later in this book. Buying at a Price / Sales ratio below 1 or a Price / Earnings ratio below 10 in a new industry can also significantly protect the downside.

Buying a Good Company with Demonstrated Growth in a Market Panic

This means that you look for demonstration of the company's and the industry's capability. For the purposes of this book, a market panic is a situation in which the market falls by more than 30% and when market indices, such as the Sensex or Nifty, are trading at Price / Earnings ratios below 12. Usually these market panics affect all companies, whether they are good or bad. Share prices of good companies then get beaten down to highly attractive, bargain basement levels. These market panics usually happen because of a need for liquidity and a fear psychosis rather than any fundamental problems with companies. Once you have identified good companies, as defined earlier in this chapter, one can apply the same valuations as in the first case, namely Price / Sales ratio below 1 or Price / Earnings ratio below 10 to purchase shares during a market panic. Though share prices can fall below purchase prices for a while, buying good companies at such attractive prices will generate good returns over the long run.

Buying a Good Company Experiencing Temporary Problems

Even the best of companies in the world cannot deliver outstanding results every quarter. Due to various market and execution related problems, good companies also have bad quarters. Despite the management team of a company having demonstrated the ability to consistently generate sales and profits in different market conditions, when they are experiencing a temporary problem, the market tends to punish the shares of these companies. However, for the long term buyer, this is a great purchase opportunity. The caveat, though, is that the problems should be of a temporary nature and the share price should fall sufficiently so that it is attractive enough to compensate you for the risk you are taking. Again, we apply the same ratios as earlier. Buy these companies if their shares are trading at Price / Sales ratios below 1 or Price / Earnings ratios are below 10.

Caveats

Companies That Fail to Execute

There are many examples of ventures with great potential that failed because of poor execution, poor timing, or a lack of initiative from the company's management.

One such example is Navneet Publications' online venture, conectschool.com. Connectschool.com was an internet-based school partnership programme where curriculum based interactive programmes would be delivered through e-learning courses. When Navneet announced the launch of connectschool.com in October 2000 through its 100% subsidiary Navneet Edutainment Ltd., it seemingly had great potential. In those days, Navneet Publications had a strong presence in only two states — Maharashtra and Gujarat — and was struggling to gain foothold in other parts of the country. Many analysts were of the opinion that through this venture, Navneet would reach out to more than 800,000 schools across the country in one stroke. And given Navneet's strong brands and experience, it looked possible.

In 2000, Navneet had strong brands like Vikas, Gala and Navneet, had the highest number (2,700) of active copyrighted titles in the market and 2,000 person years of teaching experience*. In addition to these strengths, Navneet had first mover advantage. But the venture turned out to be a fiasco. The website could not take off as expected as the company was not able to position and market the website properly, and the portal could not generate profits even after five years of its launch. Eventually, the subsidiary Navneet Edutainment was merged with the parent company in 2006 and the web site had to be withdrawn. Either this was a case of bad execution, or of bad timing, or just a lack of patience on the management's part. Just a few years later, another company, Educomp, focused on a similar model and similar market and delivered multibagger returns.

Another example that fits here is LML's attempted transition from a scooter maker to motorcycle maker. After the emergence of motorcycle as the preferred two-wheeler in India, scooter makers like Bajaj Auto and LML had to either shut down their

---

* Way2Wealth Research Desk, 2 April 2001.

operations or fight back by repositioning themselves as motorcycle makers. Bajaj Auto was able to successfully reposition itself and launched popular models in the motorcycle segment. LML, however, failed, mainly due to poor execution and wrong strategies. When the Indian two-wheeler market was moving from scooters to motorcycles, LML's promoters, the Singhanias, were caught up in fighting a bitter legal battle with co-promoters Piaggio over increasing their stake in the company. By the time LML could settle all the legal disputes and focus on its future course of business, the Indian two wheeler market was dominated by well established products from players like Hero Honda, Bajaj Auto, TVS Suzuki, and Escorts Yamaha. Teaming up with foreign players to launch new products was not uncommon in those days and LML too followed its competitors but its choice of partner was not correct. LML chose to join hands with Daeling, which was Honda's ex-licensee and this choice proved fatal to the company. Of the five launches planned, LML could launch only two — Adreno and Energy, both 100cc bikes targeted at Hero Honda Splendor, which was a rage in the market by then. While 60% of the two-wheeler market was dominated by bikes that targeted rural and semi-urban markets, LML chose to play the value game by targeting the remaining 40% of the urban market, which could afford to pay more for added features.* LML could not beat Hero Honda and Bajaj as it was starved of cash and suffered huge losses due to declining scooter volumes, which was then its mainstay.

If a company consistently fails to execute, it is best not to invest in it. Or, if an investment has already been made, it is best to exit and re-invest in other superior opportunities.

---

* "Re-inventing LML", Seema Shukla, *Business Today,* 06 October 2000.

Long-term Trends *versus* Flashes in the Pan

In the mid 19th century, the Californian Gold Rush was in full swing. All manner of prospectors moved to California in an attempt to make their fortunes in gold prospecting. One of the ways they tried to find gold was to put a pan in a running river in order to catch solid objects in the flow. Sometimes they found pieces of gold but most of the time they got falsely excited about glints in the pan, which turned out not to be gold. These were known as "flashes in the pan". The hunt for multibaggers is much like the hunt for gold. It produces several false flashes in the pan. It is generally prudent to first identify whether something is a long-term trend or just a flash in the pan. Flashes in the pan tend to experience brief moments in the sun but will eventually fade away, like bell-bottoms did after the 1970s, or dot-coms in the late 1990s. However, long term trends are those that are here to stay and will generate substantial growth for companies in such sectors. The challenge is to distinguish between long term trends and flashes-in-the-pan. Dot-coms were absurdly valued in the late 1990s but it was difficult for a lot of even highly informed investors not to get convinced that they were the wave of the future. On the flip side, one could have thought that motorcycles in India were a fad that would go away, but they turned out to be a lasting long term trend.

So how does one distinguish between a flash in the pan and a long term trend?

So how does one distinguish between a flash in the pan and a long term trend? It is not easy. One way to think about it is that long term trends are more likely to be created by fulfilling a felt need more efficiently. For example, the need for personal transportation was very high in India in the 1980s and 1990s. Cars were very expensive for the middle class. Scooters existed as an alternative but the license raj was still on so production was curtailed. When motorcycles made their appearance, they offered a superior product (higher fuel efficiency, greater speeds) and were being made in quantity. As a result, they took off dramatically and created a multibagger in Hero Honda. Similarly, thanks to the Indian government's attitude between the country's Independence in 1947 and the 1990s, phones were considered a luxury. So no infrastructural investment was made in telecommunications. In the 1990s, when cellular technology came to India, it offered an alternative where one could get a phone easily and the network provider could expand the network with relative ease compared to landlines. As a result, there are far more cell phones in India today than there are landlines. Thanks to the mobile phone revolution, Bharti Airtel became a multibagger. Contrast this with, say, e-Toys.com. There was probably a market for ordering toys over the Internet. But it did not solve as critical a problem as the lack of communication devices in India.

Understanding Financial Performance

Most multibaggers require tremendous patience. One of the reasons is that on the way to becoming a multibagger, a company has to pass through some intermediate stages. From an investment perspective, it does not pay to obsessively follow quarterly results. No category of potential multibaggers, whether a turnaround, a brand new business segment, or an ignored sector, will display steadily growing profits.

As an illustration, let us look at the financial performance of United Spirits Ltd. over the 7-year period from 2001 to 2007, when its top line grew steadily from a low of ₹1,134 crore in 2001 to ₹4,678 crore, a CAGR of 19%. During this period, the spirits industry's annual growth rate was just 8%. However, United Spirits' PAT trend was highly erratic. From ₹22.39 crore in 2001, PAT continuously declined to ₹13.11 crore in 2003. But by 2007, it had jumped to ₹494 crore (including extraordinary items). In spite of this erratic trend in profits, over the period from 2001 to 2008, United Spirits' stock increased in value by 63 times.

What does this example illustrate? Companies that are expanding rapidly tend to have patchy profitability and sometimes even disappointing profit growth. Looking at the quarterly performance of a company is akin to looking at a clock obsessively and complaining that time moves very slowly. Once you have developed conviction in a company's core business and its management team's ability to execute, you will need to trust them and be patient to fully capture the improvement in the business or in market conditions.

> Companies that are expanding rapidly tend to have patchy profitability and sometimes even disappointing profit growth.

At this point one may pertinently ask how it is possible to track a company's progress if we cannot rely on quarterly financial statements as an indicator. The approach I follow is to look for tangible progress in the company's core business, usually in the form of customer acquisition, new product launches, or new partnerships that can generate revenues. Follow such fundamental developments in the companies you are considering rather than obsessing about their quarterly results.

There is, however, a word of caution here. There comes a point when you will have to decide whether the company is really performing or not. If the company is only promise and no delivery, there is no point in being invested in it. If sales are not growing, you should begin to doubt the management's capability to execute.

General Market Conditions

One factor that is always worth thinking about is the general market conditions. Buying in times of great optimism rarely ever generates great returns. Buying in times of pessimism tends to produce very good returns. This book contains an entire chapter on bull and bear markets, which focuses on identifying times of optimism and pessimism. It is always better to buy during bear markets or in intermediate down trends than in bull markets.

> It is always better to buy during bear markets or in intermediate down trends than in bull markets.

To illustrate how market conditions can affect your return, consider the case of Infosys Technologies (*see* Figure 2.2). If you bought Infosys at its peak during the 2000 stock market bubble for ₹1,598.72 and held the stock all the way till 2007, ignoring the bad news around the company, the sector in which it operated, and the intervening stock market volatility, and sold it exactly at its 2007 peak of ₹2,366.25, then you would have earned a return of just 48%. In contrast, if you had bought the same Infosys stock at its bottom during the 2001 crash for ₹296.56 and sold it at the 2007 peak of ₹2,366.25, you would have earned a return of 697%. Not only that, post the 2001 crash, it never fell below ₹297. Its lowest point post the 2001 crash was ₹325 during 2003. This example highlights how buying in optimistic conditions generates sub-optimal returns. The knack of buying good companies when others are selling in a frenzied panic has to be developed in order to generate multibagger returns.

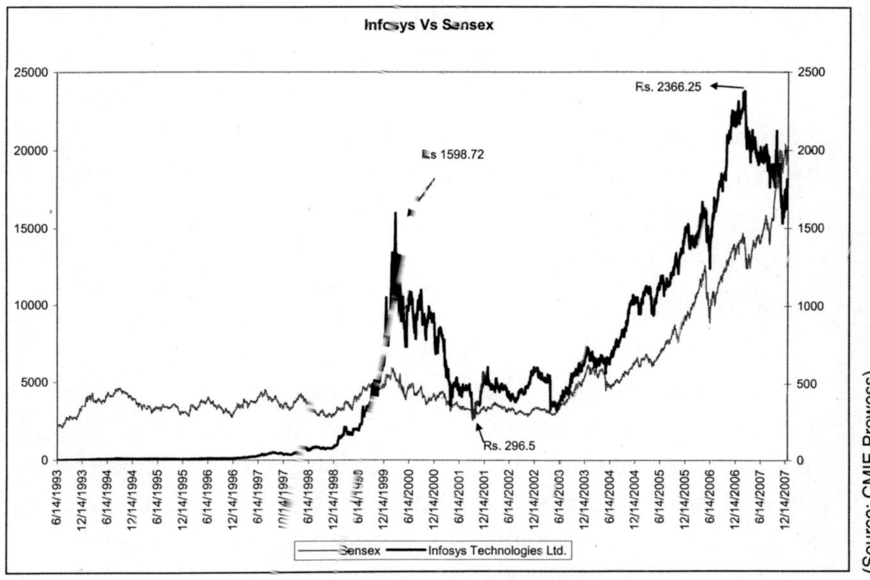

(Source: CMIE Prowess)

Figure 2.2: **How buying during market downturns boosts returns**

Liquidity and Multibaggers

Most potential multibaggers tend to have very low liquidity. Let this not deter you. By the time a stock becomes very liquid, the potential for dramatic returns would have diminished significantly. Moreover, low liquidity is a sign of lack of wider recognition. Indeed, it can be daunting to enter illiquid stocks if you need your money in a hurry. So commit only such portion of your capital to multibaggers that you can afford to have locked up for a while.

This chapter has provided you with a framework for identifying multibaggers. The core concept for identification of multibaggers is very simple: finding unrecognized change. Once you have identified unrecognized change, other factors come into play; refining the search in order to understand whether the management team can execute or if the valuation is truly low or whether market conditions are right to make a purchase. It is important to also understand that even if all these factors are present in a stock, the stock could still go down after a purchase. In a bearish environment, stocks tend to get extraordinarily cheap in spite of good fundamentals. It is always better to buy in highly pessimistic times. Markets almost always undervalue companies in such times. Once you have identified a good company that is in an attractive industry, buy aggressively in bearish times after the price damage has ceased. The courage to buy in bad times is what distinguishes the average investor from the great investor.

> The courage to buy in bad times is what distinguishes the average investor from the great investor.

3

Holding Multibaggers

> **"Success in investing doesn't correlate with I.Q. once you're above the level of 25. Once you have ordinary intelligence, what you need is the temperament to control the urges that get other people into trouble in investing."**
>
> — Warren Buffett

Almost all active investors hold potential multibaggers in their portfolio at one time or other. However, they never stay invested in the company long enough to generate a multibagger return. The reason most people cannot get multibagger returns is not because they are not intelligent enough to find potential multibaggers. It is because they are overly influenced by what other people are doing in the stock market. Thus, they behave like a part of a herd. To generate multibagger returns, you need to evaluate for yourself why the company you have invested in is falling in price and whether the fall in price is a good enough reason to sell. It is this independence of thinking that will generate multibagger returns and not extraordinary intelligence or insider information.

I quote from Warren Buffet extensively in this chapter because I think that he has mastered the attitude required to generate multibagger returns. Mr. Buffett probably disagrees with me strongly on what makes a good investment. However, Warren Buffett has no equal in his attitude towards stocks. Everyone can learn something from him and I urge you to read everything that he has written.

In the middle of bull markets, professional investors are often asked the question: “What stocks can I buy that will double in the next one year?” Unfortunately, most professionals can’t answer that question any more accurately than amateurs. However, if you increase the time frame embedded in that question to, say, ten years, the accuracy of answers becomes much higher. Not only can you answer with more confidence but you can also put a higher return expectation. In fact, a properly selected stock that is held for ten years has a high chance of becoming a multibagger.

Before we jump headlong into the process of holding a multibagger, let us examine what creates a multibagger return. A multibagger return from a properly selected company is created in three parts:

- **Attractive Purchase Price:** The stock has to be purchased at a price that is very low in comparison to its market opportunity. This only occurs when the market does not recognize the potential of the company, or if prices are artificially depressed due to overall market conditions.
- **Improvement in Company’s Fundamentals:** For the stock price to appreciate, the market needs to start seeing fundamental performance that is better than what is reflected in the stock’s price. As the company’s fundamental performance improves, its stock price tends to move in line with improved earnings and / or sales.

- **Re-rating and Market Excess:** In the third phase, a lot of people recognize that the company is a strong performer, several brokers start covering the stock, the stock's P/E multiple rises dramatically and its liquidity greatly improves.

The key change that occurs in the stock market from the first to the third phase is the Price / Earnings re-rating. So you have two factors working in your favour:

- Company's steadily improving fundamental performance, as well as
- A higher P/E ratio.

For example, let us say you have identified and purchased a company that has an EPS of ₹1 in the first phase and a P/E of 5, which means it has a stock price of ₹5. Suppose it grows its earnings by 25% every year. In ten years time, it would then have an EPS of ₹9.3. If the market recognizes its performance and re-rates the P/E to 20, the stock will have a price of ₹186. In 10 years, you would then have made a return of 37 times your original investment. Generating a multibagger is that simple. The trick is to be very diligent in doing your research. Once you have identified all the characteristics of a multibagger in a stock that is attractively priced, your innate laziness should take over. If you exit before the company grows to the greatest extent of its profit and the P/E re-rating happens you earn a sub-optimal return. Holding on tight to good companies, in spite of intervening volatility, is what generates great returns. But this is easier said than done.

Holding on tight to good companies, in spite of intervening volatility, is what generates great returns.

In this chapter, we will examine the difficulties of the holding period and the attitude one should have after purchasing a stock that you believe will become a multibagger.

Holding Period

As Warren Buffett puts it in his inimitable style, "Time is the friend of the wonderful company, the enemy of the mediocre."

The first question that comes to most people's mind is: "How long do I need to hold a stock to generate a multibagger return?" The most accurate answer is: "Longer than you think."

Most good companies tend to take between 5 and 12 years to generate extraordinary returns. If one has the unique knack of buying at the bottom of the market, or just before a big rally starts, which very few investors do, it is possible to shorten this time frame significantly. The question of holding also becomes highly relevant if you find other opportunities that you consider extraordinary. If there are alternate investment opportunities that can generate a higher return than a particular stock that you are holding, then you may want to cut short your holding period in order to take up the other opportunity. However, there is no right answer to this question. One should hold on as long as the company is performing well and growth is not stagnating, assuming that you have bought the stock at a reasonable price.

Our research confirms that multibaggers are not created overnight. Even though 80% of a stock's gain may come in 20% of the time period for which it is held, it is very difficult to time to perfection and buy only stocks that go up as soon as they are bought. The probability that a properly selected stock will go up is increased dramatically when it is held for at least five years. The return comes in fits and starts and those who try to buy only when a stock is going up end up catching very small parts of the gain. Sometimes they also lose a significant amount of capital trying to time the purchase too finely and minimize their holding period.

Volatility

> **"A public opinion poll is no substitute for thought."**
> — Warren Buffett

Volatility is a key feature of the stock market. Prices swing wildly both on the upside and on the downside. Emerging markets like India are particularly "irrational" and swing violently due to various reasons. Specific stocks tend to swing even more than the stock market indices. In this section, we will try to understand why price swings are created. Understanding this will make it easier for investors to decide when they should hold and when they should sell because volatility by itself is usually not a reason to sell a properly selected stock.

Very simply put, volatility is created because of the herd-like mentality of most investors in the markets. Investors are very afraid of notional losses. Some investment vehicles, such as hedge funds, are expected to deliver positive returns in all market conditions. Since the investors in these hedge funds are always comparing their performance against a benchmark index, they also turn blind buy ers in an uptrend. This attitude tends to exaggerate volatility that is already inherent in the market. The key to generating multibagger returns is to understand whether price movements actually reflect the underlying fundamentals.

> Volatility is created because of the herd-like mentality of most investors in the markets. Investors are very afraid of notional losses.

Let us delve deeper into price swings. Why do investors behave like herds? Why are price movements so exaggerated in either direction? Do fundamentals vary so much that prices change so dramatically? Volatility is created more often by liquidity demand and supply rather than due to any fundamentals of the stock or the market. In plain English, liquidity translates to cash. Liquidity demand means that there is a demand for cash. Conversely, liquidity supply means that there is demand for assets. Since there are investors of every type with differing horizons and different liquidity needs in the market, demand and supply of liquidity happens at various points. For example, when there is a sudden downtrend in global markets, there are margin calls on hedge funds. These funds then have to sell a lot of the assets they have in order to generate cash. They become liquidity demanders in such a market. Similarly, a lot of Indian individual investors try to use futures as a means for taking large positions in the markets. As soon as there is a down-turn and hedge funds sell, Indian futures traders have to liquidate their positions to generate cash to meet their own margin calls. Some other investors tend to set stop losses on their positions. This means that sell orders will automatically be executed when the price drops below a pre-defined point. This results in even higher volatility. It is important to understand that volatility in its stock price does not necessarily mean that the company's fundamentals have deteriorated. Unless one has this insight, it is impossible to participate profitably in equity markets over the long term.

It is important to understand that volatility in its stock price does not necessarily mean that the company's fundamentals have deteriorated.

Volatility is scary for most investors. However, price volatility creates fantastic opportunities for the long term buyer. In fact, my opinion is that volatility should be taken advantage of and not feared. Let us see some examples of volatility in stocks that have generated multibagger returns.

A case in point is Bharat Earth Movers Ltd (*see* Figure 3.1). From its 2000 bottom of ₹14 to its 2008 peak of about ₹1,700, the stock delivered more than a 100-fold return. However, from its peak in 2000 to its trough in 2001, it fell more than 50%. In 2001, it subsequently rallied to ₹31 and then suddenly fell off to ₹12.65 in early 2002. It again rallied to ₹100 in 2002 and lost more than 50% to fall to ₹48 in 2003. From the ₹48 bottom in 2003, it rallied to a peak of ₹247 in 2004. It then corrected by 58% to ₹102. From its ₹102 bottom in 2004, BEML rallied to ₹1,730 in 2006. It then corrected by nearly 50% to ₹830 in the same year. By December 2007, it rallied back up to ₹1,800 only to suffer another fall in January 2008. This is only one example of the kind of volatility one can experience.

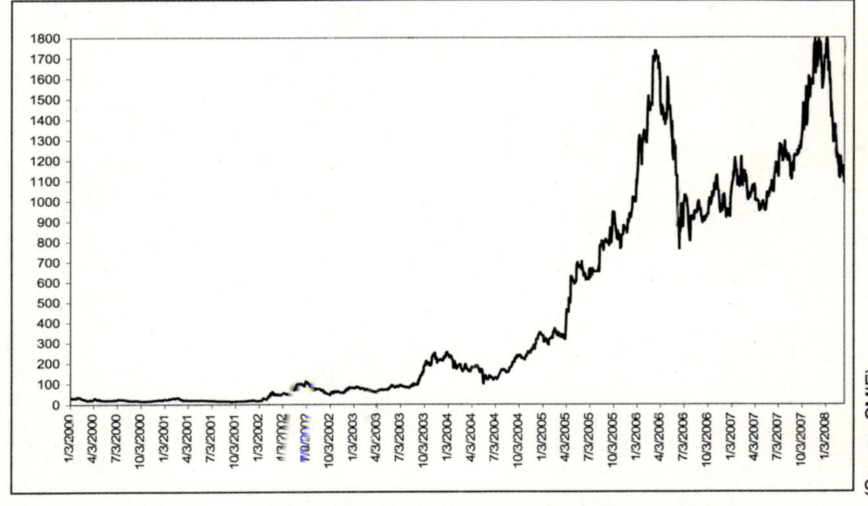

(Source: CMIE)

Figure 3.1: **Volatility in their share prices is a common feature of multibaggers**

Let us now consider the example of Hero Honda (*see* Figure 3.2). If you bought Hero Honda in February 1993, the stock immediately corrected by 25% to ₹9 by March. Bottoming out at ₹9, the stock ran up to ₹46 by August 1994. By November 1995, the stock lost 59% to end up at ₹18.5. Most investors would have been very rattled by this then and would probably have exited. From the November 1995 bottom, the stock started a relentless rally that drove its price up to ₹130 by May 1998. The stock then corrected viciously to ₹85 by June 1998, a fall of nearly 35%. From that bottom, the stock rallied to a high of ₹280 by August 1999, only to fall to ₹116, losing 60% of its value, by April 2001. From its 2001 low, Hero Honda rallied up to a high of ₹380 in March 2002, only to give up a lot of its gains, lose 48% of its value and settle down at ₹195.

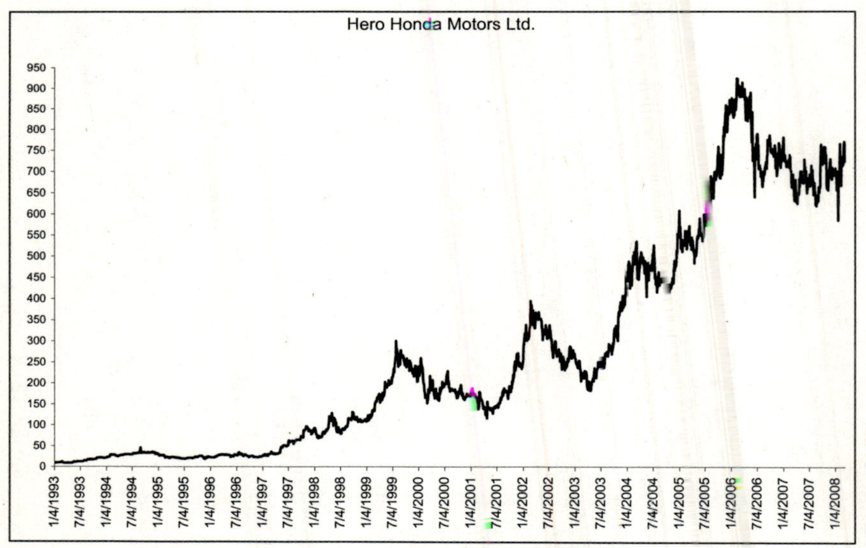

Figure 3.2: **Volatility in a multibagger's share price is no reason to sell**

From this low, the stock rose to ₹890 by March 2006. An investor who held the stock from 1993 would have made nearly 100 times his money. But holding Hero Honda would have been akin to a motorcycle ride with no shock absorbers on an unpaved village road.

These are only two examples out of the many companies that were examined in the research effort for this book. Almost every stock that has been a multibagger has given its investors a very rocky ride. Multibaggers have lost between 30% and 75% of their value from time to time. Only those investors who bought right and stuck to their guns made extraordinary returns. Those who panicked and sold at every fall made mediocre returns.

Types of Sell-offs

There are broadly three types of sell-offs.

Market-Wide Sell-off

This means that, for some reason, the overall market turns down and all stocks, irrespective of their fundamentals, lose value. In recent times, such market weakness occurred in India in 1994, 1998, 2000, 2003, 2006 and 2008. To see the effect of a market-wide sell-off on a specific stock, let us consider the example of Pantaloon Retail. The company is in an under-penetrated, high growth industry. Its sales and profit growth in March 2006 quarter was at 66% and 52% compared to the corresponding quarter in the previous year (*see* Table 3.1). But the market fall in May 2006 (*see* Figure 3.3) triggered its stock price to slide from ₹385 to ₹228 (a 40% decline). The market decided to ignore the fundamentals of the company and sold it mercilessly.

Table 3.1

Performance Indicators of Pantaloon Retail

Amount in ₹cr

Year	*Sales*	*PAT*	*Year*	*Sales*	*PAT*	*Year*	*Sales*	*PAT*
Dec-04	239.11	10.14	Mar-05	275.3	10.68	Jun-05	360.15	10.79
Dec-05	472.44	18.56	Mar-06	455.9	16.24	Jun-06	578.12	15.83
Change (%)	98%	83%	Change (%)	66%	52%	Change (%)	61%	47%

(*Source:* CMIE)

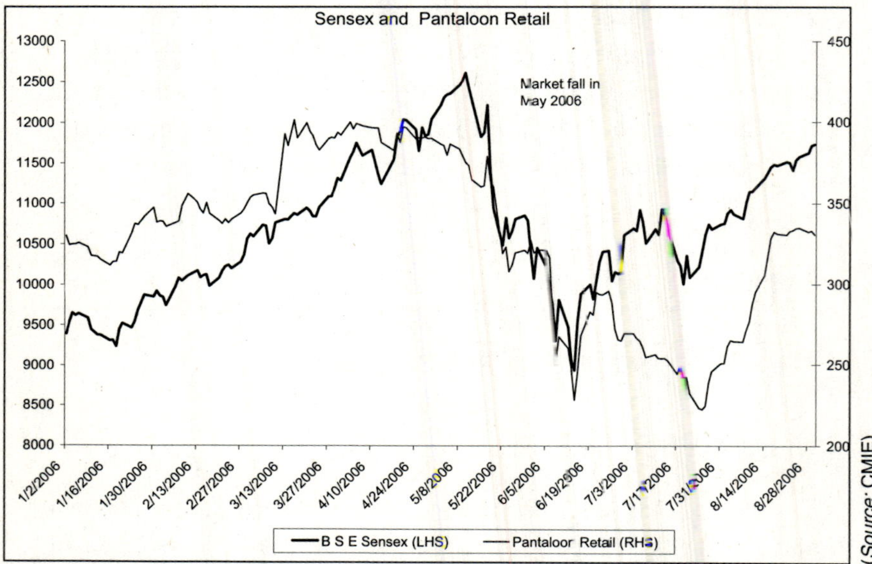

(*Source:* CMIE)

Figure 3.3: **Market-wide sell-offs may have temporary adverse effects even on multibagger stocks, as happened with Pantaloon in 2006**

Sectoral Sell-off

Sometimes, the market singles out a specific sector for punishment. The Indian midcap IT space in 2007-2008 is a great example. The rise of the rupee adversely affected these companies and several of them lost between 50% and 80% of their 2007 peak values (*see* Figure 3.4).

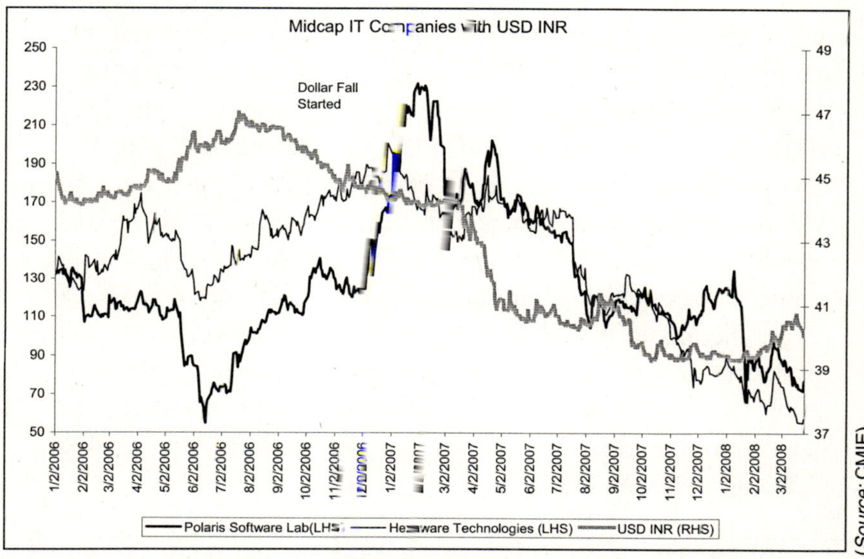

(*Source:* CMIE)

Figure 3.4: **A sectoral sell-off will temporarily drag down prices even of companies which are performing well**

Company-Specific Sell-off

Sometimes, a company sees significant diminution its in stock price because it performs less well than was expected by the market, or it gives lower guidance than what the market anticipated. Sometimes, factors like a fire in a plant or disruption of production or adverse government regulations can also impact a single company. Sometimes a company's stock price is bid up in anticipation of a merger or acquisition and when this does not materialize, the price of its shares falls substantially. In recent times, we saw such company specific sell-offs in India when a domestic company acquired a foreign company because investors were afraid that the Indian acquirer was overpaying.

Let us consider the example of Tata Steel acquisition of the Anglo Dutch Steel giant, Corus. Tata Steel's final bid for Corus at an enterprise value of over \$13 billion worked out to a multiple of approximately 7 times EBITDA (earnings before interest, tax, depreciation and amortization) for the year ended 31 December 2005 and 9 times for the 12 months to 30 September 2006. The market felt that this was much higher than 5.5–6 times paid by Mittals for Arcelor and the stock went down from ₹534 to ₹413 (*see* Figure 3.5). But the merged entity became the largest steel player in India and the 6th largest in the world with a presence across the globe. It also emerged as one of the lowest cost steel producers in the world with a strong product portfolio and technology. Later, once the market recognized the synergies between the two companies, Tata Steel's stock price went up to ₹990 (138% up from the lows).

(*Source:* CMIE)

Figure 3.5: **The stock price of Tata Steel fell in 2006 as the market was initially not impressed by its large acquisition of Corus**

Causes of Sell-offs

There are several occasions where the market turns viciously downward. In fact, in 2008-09 we witnessed a series of such brutal sell-offs in the Indian market. It is important to understand that market weakness sometimes has no fundamental basis. The market sells off primarily because of leverage, sentiment and psychology. However, if the market as a whole is overvalued, the market may sell off on account of its own weight. Let us examine the role of each of these factors in market sell-offs.

Leverage

Fortunately or unfortunately, all liquid markets tend to have people who believe that they can enhance their returns by using leverage. In the Indian context, leveraged players include high net worth individuals as well as foreign hedge funds. Most Indian institutional investors do not employ leverage. Except for the most skilled of market participants, most people actually end up losing money because of leverage. As it relates to the stock market, leverage means that you borrow money in order to purchase more shares than you can afford to with your own resources. In order to access this leverage, a borrower has to pledge his shares to the lender. With money received from the lender, he purchases more shares. If his shares go up, the borrower is able to sell his shares and retain the profit on both the shares purchased with his own money as well as those purchased with the borrowed money. If, however, his shares go down the trouble starts. In such a case, he has to deposit additional collateral with the lender. If the shares he has purchased go down significantly, he has to meet margin calls to

> The most dramatic stock corrections occur because of leverage.

make good the difference between his purchase price and the price that the shares trade at presently. If he does not have the cash to meet this margin call, he is forced to sell shares. So whenever the market turns down suddenly, a lot of people are forced to liquidate their positions in order to meet margin calls. This creates a cascade effect where others have to sell because of the downward pressure on share prices that one sell-off creates. A chain reaction thus occurs where all shares fall in price because of the leverage existing in the system until all the leverage is wiped out. The most dramatic stock corrections occur because of this reason — leverage.

A great recent example of how leverage can work against a stock is Orchid Chemicals. On 15 March 2008, the stock went into a free fall (*see* Figure 3.6). It was down by 44% from the previous trading day. The reason for such a sharp fall was initially assumed to be because of selling by Bear Stearns, which was unwinding its positions because of its own financial problems. But the fall was greatly aggravated by the leveraged position taken by the founder and managing director of the company Kailasam Raghvendra Rao. Apparently, in 2007 Mr. Rao had borrowed a sum of ₹85 crore from Indiabulls and Religare Finvest to increase his stake in the company from 17% to 24%. The March 2008 sell-off forced Bear Stearns to exit, which then forced Mr. Rao to sell his shares. He made a personal loss of close to ₹75 crore due to the sale of his company's share in the open market by the lenders. Did this have anything to do with the fundamentals of Orchid Chemicals? Probably not. Orchid fantastically illustrates the viciousness of leverage in a falling market.

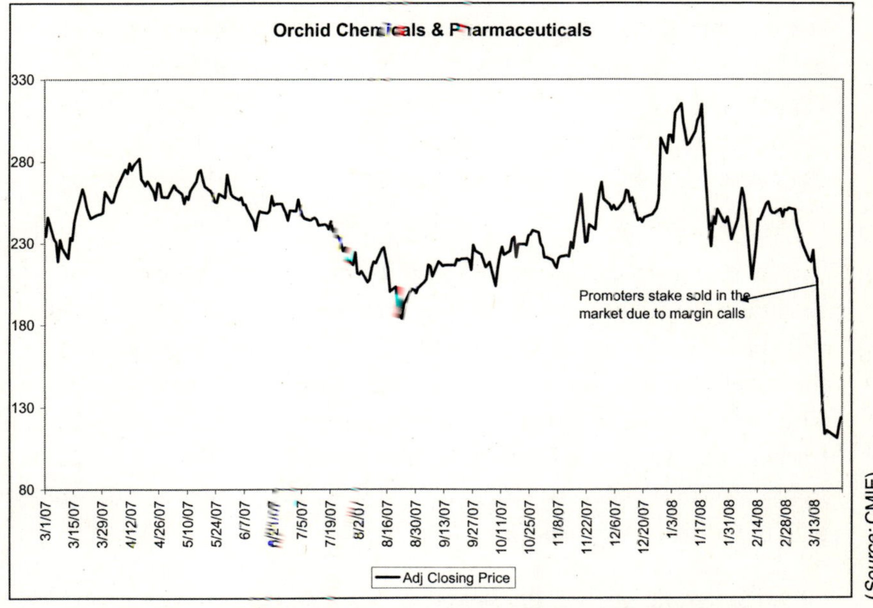

(Source: CMIE)

Figure 3.6: **The stock price of Orchid Chemicals and Pharmaceuticals plummeted when promoter stakes were sold due to excess leverage**

Psychology

Stock markets as a whole, or prices of individual shares, also sometimes fall precipitously because of the nervous psychology of investors. Even unleveraged investors get panicky when they see their shares lose a lot of value. So they decide to get out of their positions in a hurry by selling their shares. This creates further declines because those who have leverage will also be forced to sell as the unleveraged players sell their positions.

Overvaluation

Individual stocks as well as the entire stock market sometimes get overvalued. When prices are extremely high in relation to the fundamentals, expectations of performance from companies also get raised very high. If companies fail to deliver on these expectations, people sell such overvalued stocks immediately. Since leveraged positions are very high in most bubble situations, the de-leveraging process and psychology take a toll on market prices.

The best example of this was Zee Telefilms in the year 2000. The company was trading at a P/E multiple of 757 and had a market capitalization of ₹60,000 crore when the estimated size of the media business in India as a whole was only ₹10,000 crore. This was a great sell signal at the valuations that the stock was trading; the stock then plummeted from its highs of ₹1,555 on 24 February 2000, and reached a level of ₹387 on 8 August 2000 — a 75% fall from the peak!

Poor Financial Performance or Guidance

Individual stocks can experience a sell off even when there is no market-wide sell-off if their future guidance suggests lower performance or if their quarterly numbers are poor. A good example was the technology leader Infosys Technologies in 2003. The company's weaker-than-expected performance coupled with gloomier profit guidance for the year ahead knocked the wind out of the stock price. The company's profit guidance of about 12.5% year-on-year fell short of market expectations of 18 per cent, which led the stock price to fall by ₹1,113.45 or 27 per cent from the previous day's close.

Poor Economic Conditions

Sometimes, macroeconomic factors have a huge influence on market performance. Markets tend to sell off if they receive poor news about economic growth, inflation, interest rates or several other such factors.

Reacting to Sell-offs

There are only three major reasons to sell a properly selected stock:

1. Overvaluation,
2. Permanent adverse developments which a management cannot innovate its way out of, or
3. If the original reason for making the investment is no longer valid.

If none of these three criteria are met, there is no reason to even consider selling the stock. This section will outline how one should react to each type of sell-off.

Reacting to Market-Wide Sell-offs

> **"The future is never clear, and you pay a very high price in the stock market for a cheery consensus. Uncertainty is the friend of the buyer of long-term values."** — Warren Buffett

Let us now assume you are holding shares in a company and you do not have any leverage.

If a vicious market-wide sell-off begins, the question you should ask yourself is whether the fall in price is because some over-leveraged hedge fund is selling and whether this will alter the fundamentals of the company. In most cases, the fall in share prices rarely ever alter a company's fundamentals. If you believe the fundamentals of the company are good and that they will continue to grow their sales and earnings in the long term, there is no reason to actually sell. In fact, you may want to add to your position.

> In most cases, the fall in share prices rarely ever alter a company's fundamentals.

One caveat, however: some capital-hungry companies are dependent on growing their businesses with fresh capital that is raised through equity markets. If the equity market tanks, they will not be able to raise capital and their growth plans will get affected. You may want to think twice if you are holding such a company. But in the long term, equity markets tend to go up and they will again be able to raise capital at good prices at some point in the future. If you are holding a capital-hungry business, it is best to assess the situation carefully and then decide whether to continue holding or to sell.

Similarly, if the market sentiment is poor and everyone you know is dumping stocks, you need to ask yourself if the fundamentals of your company are going to be affected because your neighbour or friend is selling his stocks. If the fundamentals are not affected by such a sell-off, there is no need to worry.

While temporary economic slowdowns may sometimes be anticipated by the market, more often than not, negative stock market performance will not negatively impact the economy; it sometimes does so only if capital dries up completely. So a slowing economy is not a reason to sell stocks. Moreover, unless the economy is poorly managed, economic performance eventually picks up if the structural environment is good. I would argue that the Indian economy is structurally set up for good performance for the long term. Sell-offs created by economic data should not be any cause for panic.

Reacting to Stock Specific Sell-offs

Sometimes, even potential multibagger stocks that are picked using the framework outlined in this book tend to perform poorly. It is not at all unusual to see very good companies deliver one quarter, or even one year, of poor sales or earnings. In the complicated world we live in, there can be several reasons for such poor performance: either a product performs poorly, or production is affected due to a disruption in the plant, or the market conditions are not good in a particular quarter. The stock market tends to react very sharply to such earnings disappointments. When such poor performance occurs, it is important to ask oneself if the long-term opportunity for the company is still intact. If it is, a quarter, or even a year, of poor earnings may actually be a great time to buy more stock. If, however, you believe that further growth cannot occur in these companies due to any reason, it may be better for you to exit the stock and find other investment opportunities. But no successful long term investor has grown rich by fretting over quarterly data and forgetting the larger opportunity. In fact, some of the best returns have been delivered by companies whose quarterly performance was somewhat patchy. Pantaloon, United Spirits, BEML, all have had poor quarters and resultant sell-offs. But anyone who buys or sells such a stock based on every quarterly report is unlikely to capture the extraordinary returns that these stocks have offered.

The price performance of REI Agro, the basmati rice processing and marketing company, illustrates the above point. The company could not deliver good results, though the prices of agri commodities like rice were in a bull phase, and its sales declined for the three consecutive quarters in 2006 (*see* Table 3.2). This led to a drop in the company's share price from ₹192.5 in

Table 3.2

REI Agro's 3 Bad Quarters

Amount in ₹Cr					
Year	*Sales*	*Year*	*Sales*	*Year*	*Sales*
Mar-05	250.73	Jun-05	301.32	Sep-05	275.1
Mar-06	216.42	Jun-06	235.43	Sep-06	240.24
Change (%)	-14%	Change (%)	-22%	Change (%)	-13%

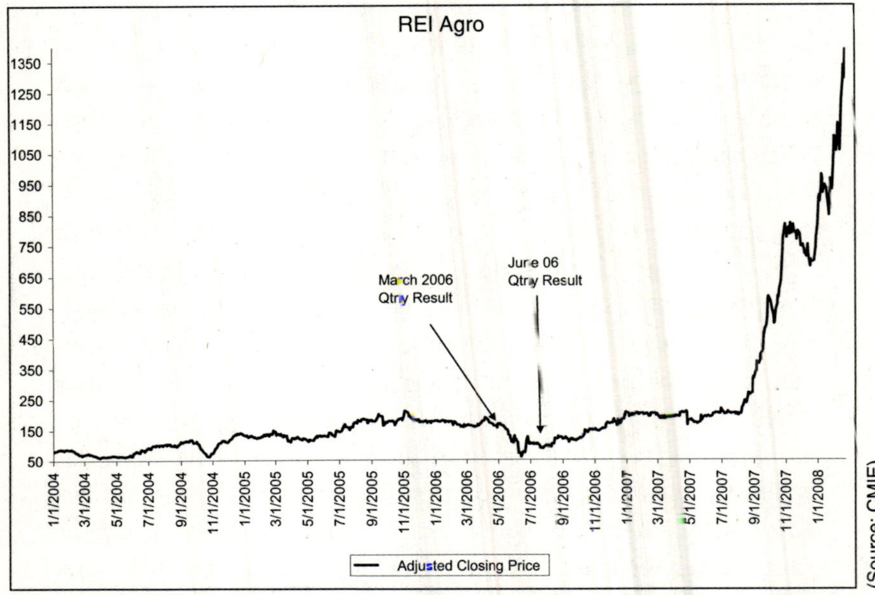

Figure 3.7: **Don't let your judgement about a likely multibagger be overly affected by a few bad quarters. See how REI Agro's price recovered very sharply once the market understood that the company had overcome the three bad quarters it faced in 2006.**

April 2006 to ₹60 by June 2006 (*see* Figure3.7). The price could not reclaim its previous highs till December 2006. After that, the stock reached a lifetime high ₹1,500 in March 2008.

Typically, a management's capability to execute comes into question when quarterly or annual numbers are consistently poor. When this happens, it is necessary to understand what went wrong. Sometimes, it may be a plant shutdown, or an adverse movement in a currency or some other factor completely beyond the management's control. In such cases, it makes no sense to sell the stock unless you believe that the poor financial performance is going to be a recurring feature due to some long-term changes in the business that the company is in. At other times, such as, an accident in a plant or difficulty in growth in one quarter, it may just be a temporary phenomenon. Developing the judgment to identify whether poor performance is temporary or permanent is essential in order to be able to decide whether to buy, hold or sell. You must investigate whether the poor performance was because of temporary factors that were out of the management's control in order to be able to judge whether to stay in, add, or get out. If in your judgement management has lost its touch, it is best to get out. But it pays to stick with a management team that has demonstrated great growth in the past.

Reacting to Sectoral Sell-offs

Sometimes, an entire sector experiences a sell-off. Usually, this is because of an adverse development specific to the sector. Examples of this include the Indian IT sector sell-off in 2007-08 as the rupee rallied against the dollar. At other times, a sectoral sell-off can be triggered by government regulation. All sugar stocks sold off dramatically between 2006 and 2007 after the Indian government intervened in the pricing of sugar as well as the minimum support

> For multibagger hunters it is best to avoid sectors with too much government intervention.

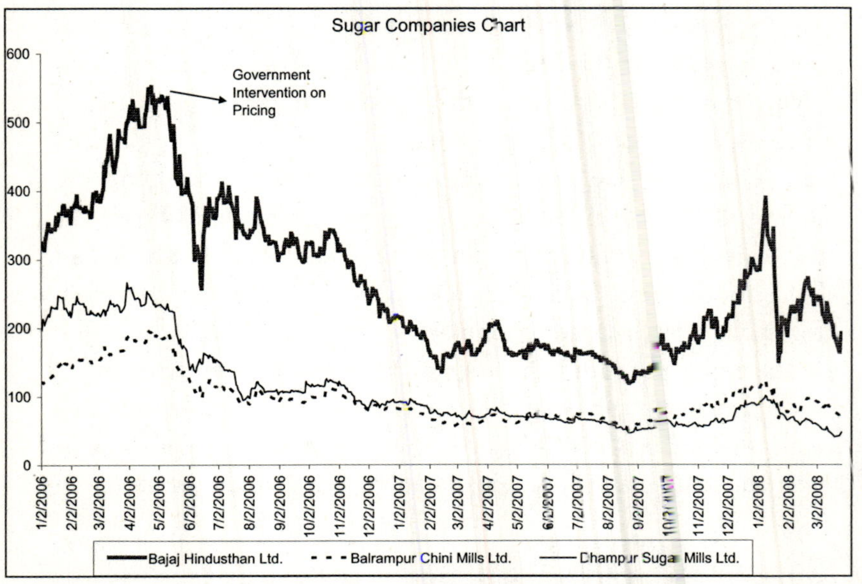

Figure 3.8: **Sometimes sectoral sell-offs are triggered by sector-adverse developments. The sugar industry was badly affected by the government's intervention in sugar pricing. It is usually best to avoid industries which the government is prone to intervene in.**

price for sugarcane farmers (*see* Figure 3.8). Similarly, the entire oil marketing sector comes under pressure whenever the government refuses to allow these companies to charge a fair retail price for petroleum products. As a result, these companies did not perform in the 2003-08 bull market at all.

For multibagger hunters it is best to avoid sectors with too much government intervention. If the government can unduly influence the price of the product being sold by a company through diktat, it is not worth being invested in the company. However, there are some sectors, such as mobile communications, where the telecom regulatory authority has put downward pressure on prices and yet was unable to stop these companies from performing well. So there is no hard and fast rule but in my experience, it is not profitable to bet against a populist government. However, when the sectoral sell-off is due to factors other than government intervention, it is worth examining the following three factors.

Is the Adverse Development Permanent?

For example, if one has a view on the exchange rate of the rupee against the dollar, one could argue that the rupee is in a secular uptrend against the dollar. That would mean that Indian IT companies which are dependant on dollar denominated contracts will lose their lustre.

Is It In the Price?

Sometimes the price correction is so steep that any positive development can result in a dramatic and long term up move in the stock. There were some stocks, which in the 2008-09 correction, fell to levels below the level of cash on their balance sheets! If such a company is debt free, it means that we are getting the operations of the company for free! Such situations merit investigation with intent to invest, assuming that all the other factors we look for in multibaggers are still present in a stock. Look for market prices to fall below some tangible value (such as book value or value of assets or replacement value of assets) in such sell-offs if the company continues to have other characteristics of a good company. When such an opportunity presents itself, and the original investment case is not violated, one should buy with both hands.

Is the Management Capable of Turning the Situation Around?

This is the most important question to ask. Capable managements can find ways around the knottiest of problems. If the management team has survived adversity in the past and come out on top, it is usually an indication that they may be able to do it again. Understanding if the company has successfully changed a business model or business plan to suit new circumstances is absolutely essential in order to generate confidence in management. Looking at financial performance can also give you a clue. In the past, has the company's financial performance bounced back after a period of adversity? If it has, it means that the management was able to tackle the issues presented by a negative development. Knowing what the company is presently doing to address the challenges it faces also gives you a clue to deduce whether the management is capable or not. Using all these tools, if you have confidence in the management, it is worth staying invested even if there is a permanent adverse development in the business that the company is in because the management may find a way to get the business back its earning power.

Ideally, if the adverse development is temporary, it is worth holding on to the stock. If the adverse development is permanent, it may be best to sell the stock before it falls precipitously. However, you should evaluate the capability of management to change the business model of the company to thrive in a new business environment before you sell. If you have faith in the management, then it is worth holding the stock — and perhaps even adding more of the stock to your portfolio after it falls.

Dealing with Overvaluation

Overvaluation is the most difficult situation to describe and deal with. Once a stock gets overvalued, it can continue to go up even though there is no more value left in it. How far to ride such a stock is then the difficult question to answer. But if a stock starts falling, and you believe that it is in overvalued territory, it should be sold.

A thorny question at this point is: what is overvaluation? A company can be overvalued either intrinsically or extrinsically.

Intrinsic overvaluation is what text books define as overvaluation. That is, a discounted cash flow will show that the company cannot produce enough cash flows to justify its market price. However, in very fast growing companies, discounted cash flow is meaningless. Simple traditional valuation ratios can be of some help. A Price / Earnings (P/E) ratio of over 60 on real earnings can generally be considered overvalued. By "real earnings" I mean earnings that are substantial and not very small. In the case of turnarounds or start-ups, earnings tend to be very small since the company is on the verge of growing its sales dramatically and is on its way to earning more profits. This small level of profits results in abnormally high P/E ratios for startups and turnarounds. Real earnings are profits of established companies that have shown consistent profitability in the past and are not in a turnaround or startup phase.

Similarly a Price / Sales (P/S) ratio of over 10 is overvalued. Just because these metrics are breached does not mean that a stock will not go up. Overvaluation and irrationality are in the very nature of the market. But when these ratios are breached, it is worth being cautious and ready to sell if you believe that the price move is not sustainable.

Traditional valuation ratios alone cannot be used to make buy / hold / sell decision because they are notoriously unreliable as indicators of potential growth. This is when the concept of extrinsic valuation helps.

Extrinsic valuation, simply defined, is ratio of the market capitalization to the value of the opportunity. At this point, it has to be conceded that the value of the opportunity can be very inaccurate and subjective. But, generally, a back-of-the-envelope calculation should give you a rough cut estimate of the market opportunity. If the market capitalization of the company is more than 25% of that market opportunity, I would argue that it is extrinsically overvalued. The key point to also take away is that your estimate of the market opportunity may also change, depending on the changing situation. It can either go up or down. If you see extrinsic overvaluation, it is time to get ready to sell the stock if you perceive a sudden and deep fall.

Coping with Gains and Losses in Your Stocks

A buy / sell / hold decision should never be dependent on whether a stock shows a gain or a loss while you are holding it. If the initial conditions for making your investment are still valid, you should stay invested and endeavour to add a stock that has fallen in price because it allows you to buy the same opportunity at a cheaper price. Obsession with your own gain or loss will result in completely sub-optimal buy / sell decisions. In addition, it will increase your transaction costs and taxes. But it takes several years for anyone in the stock market to learn that once a purchase decision after diligence has been done, it is best to stay invested as long as the original investment thesis continues to hold. It is best to ignore your profit or loss on a stock after you have purchased it if you are confident that you have purchased the right company.

In sum, if you have done a good job of identifying a potential multibagger, and the original case for investing in it has not changed, adverse price movements present an opportunity to add more to your position. This is true of most cases except when the stock becomes intrinsically and extrinsically overvalued. Not only are your returns improve if you follow this method, but your transaction costs and taxes are lower.

4

When to Sell

The decision to sell a stock is much more difficult than the decision to buy or to hold it. There are times when an overvalued stock gets even more overvalued and makes a seller regret his decision to sell. At other times, dramatic price falls can shake confidence in an investment and make it tempting to sell when the price still has a lot more upside left. Rare is the selling decision that a seller has not re-considered at some point or the other. However, the key to a happy life is to consider each sub-optimal sell decision a learning experience.

I am going to try to give a framework for making a selling decision. As with buying, dealing with the aftermath of selling is as important as the actual process of selling.

Why Sell?

Warren Buffett tells us that his favourite holding period is "forever". Then why not just buy something we like and then hold it forever? The answer is very simple: plans don't always work out. The original promise in a company may not play out as one expected. There may be new technologies or consumer preferences that queer the pitch for a company. Sometimes, we identify a great sector but pick the wrong stock. Other times, a management loses steam and fails to perform in spite of great performance by the industry. Sometimes, the global situation changes dramatically. Anything can happen. Selling under the circumstances mentioned above preserves capital.

At other times we have to sell in order to take advantage of the great, and sometimes absurd, price that the market offers for our investments. The price the market offers at times can be completely irrational. At prices like that, it is best to sell and look for other opportunities to invest your gains in. The selling decision here is based on the high valuations that the market is giving to your holdings as well as signs that the market is very euphoric. As I have mentioned elsewhere in this book, understanding signs of euphoria and despair are both necessary for making buy / sell decisions. It is almost always best to sell into euphoria. To understand both sell cases, let us look deeper both into selling to preserve capital as well as selling to book profits.

Selling to Protect Capital

As noted earlier, sometimes it is better to sell a company that is not performing up to the mark rather than holding on to it in hope that it will do better. This decision has to be based on fundamental reasons, and not merely because the price is falling. The danger of making this decision is that sometimes it is easy to lose confidence in a company whose stock is falling. If the original reasons to buy are still in place, it is foolish to sell only because there is a decline in price, or because that stock shows a loss in your portfolio. The main reasons to sell a company for protecting profits are outlined below.

Technological Obsolescence

Sometimes, a company that is using or selling a specific technology will no longer be relevant if the technology changes. A simple example that is often used by Warren Buffet is the horse buggy business. The horse buggy business had to pack its bags and go away once the automobile became mainstream. Similarly, manufacturers of typewriters, such as Smith & Corona, went out of business with the advent of the personal computer.

These technological changes have to provoke responses from the management. If a management is not able to recognize or react to such changes, it is always best to sell a stock. Moreover,

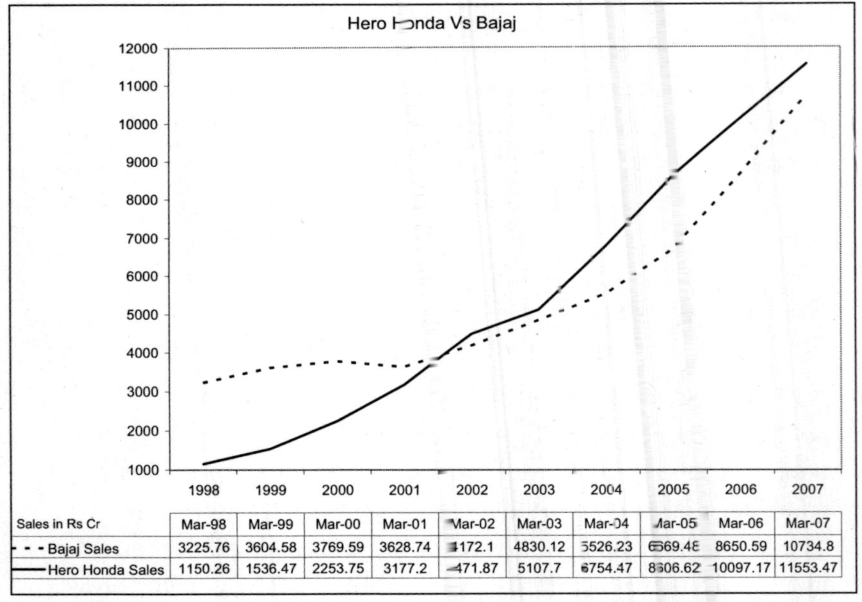

Sales in Rs Cr	Mar-98	Mar-99	Mar-00	Mar-01	Mar-02	Mar-03	Mar-04	Mar-05	Mar-06	Mar-07
Bajaj Sales	3225.76	3604.58	3769.59	3628.74	4172.1	4830.12	5526.23	6569.48	8650.59	10734.8
Hero Honda Sales	1150.26	1536.47	2253.75	3177.2	4471.87	5107.7	6754.47	8606.62	10097.17	11553.47

Figure 4.1: **Note how Hero Honda sales overtook the established Bajaj Auto as consumer preference shifted from scooters to motorcycles**

technological obsolescence is not restricted only to providers of technology; it equally impacts users of technology. Companies like Western Union, which were originally providers of telegraph services, nearly went out of business because of the fax machine before they changed their business model to money transfer services. A great example of a technology change in India was the shift from scooters to motorbikes. This resulted in Hero Honda becoming a multibagger and Bajaj Auto lagging Hero Honda for a long time. As the chart (Figure 4.1) shows, even though Bajaj had higher sales than Hero Honda until 2000, it started lagging Hero Honda from then onwards.

Poor Execution

Some companies are just better at identifying and exploiting opportunities compared to others. Sears and Walmart in the United States were both in the business of retailing and Sears was already a giant when Walmart started. Walmart was a much better retailer, though, and it became the largest company in the world whereas Sears just languished. Sears was eventually bought by Eddie Lampert, who also bought K-mart, another wounded Walmart competitor. Mr. Lampert believed that he could somehow turn these two laggards around and re-instate their former glory.

A persistent lack of growth in sales is a sure signal that the management is facing some difficulty in exploiting opportunities.

A management's inability to change shows itself in the financials of the company. Some companies just cannot grow their sales or earnings. Earnings tend to fluctuate due to various reasons, but a persistent lack of growth in sales is a sure signal that the management is facing some difficulty in exploiting opportunities. If a company cannot grow sales for more than two or three years, it is probably better to sell it rather than hold in the hope of improved sales in future.

Difficult to Exploit Opportunities

Sometimes while an opportunity looks very large, and potentially very profitable, it is very difficult for a company to truly exploit the opportunity's potential. For example, in the mid-to-late 1990s, windmills were considered a great investment opportunity. However, several companies that set up wind farms went broke because the technology was too immature and sufficient quantities of power could not be produced to meet demand. Similarly, both in the mid-1990s and in the mid-2000s, airlines were considered a huge growth industry. While the demand for travel may have been quite high, but cost dynamics, government regulation and high capital requirements led to many airlines going broke. Damania Airlines, East West, NEPC and several others shut down in the 1990s. The structure and capital requirements of this industry were quite different from what the promoters' and investors' had expected. As a result, while the opportunity looked promising, exploiting it proved very difficult and shareholders barely earned any returns.

Sometimes, over-optimistic assessments of demand are made when a new product or technology is introduced. One such opportunity was aqua-farms in the early 1990s. The opportunity was not as large as originally envisaged and most entrants burnt their fingers. The same held true for a lot of dot-com ventures in the late 1990s. So it is important to understand whether the envisaged opportunity is actually being exploited or is proving "unexploitable" by companies within that industry. When an opportunity proves too difficult to exploit, it is best to exit companies that are targeting that opportunity.

Events Materially Change the Opportunity

Some industries are inordinately affected by government intervention, economic developments, or the failure of key clients. Strong companies with big balance sheets can usually weather a lot of storms and come up smelling roses but companies with weaker balance sheets can rarely survive big events. The petroleum retailing business in India is a great example. With great fanfare, Reliance launched its petroleum retail venture with beautiful petrol pumps and the latest technology. But the government controlled the retail price of petroleum for the public sector oil marketing companies, effectively capping the retail price of petrol and diesel. No private retailer of these products could compete with the prices offered by public sector companies. The government was not interested in subsidizing the private sector. This resulted in Reliance, at least temporarily, abandoning this venture. Similarly, the government tends to intervene in politically sensitive commodities, like sugar. Sugar companies' P&Ls and their stock prices tend to fluctuate wildly with announcements from the government as well as court rulings on the minimum support price of sugarcane.

The 2008 credit crisis in the US is a great example of how economic or financial developments can affect companies. As a result of the bursting of the credit bubble, even large, well-established companies like Bear Stearns, Lehman Brothers and AIG went bankrupt. Several home builders also went out of business and mortgage lenders suffered severe damage to their balance sheets. The P&Ls of exporters to the US became very fragile because of this credit crisis. A lot of Indian exporters with weak balance sheets may have suffered irrevocable damage because of the crisis in the United States. Such events can change the fortunes of some companies and industries. When such events occur, it is important to understand the nature of their impact. If there is a permanent adverse impact on a company you are holding, it is better to sell your investment and preserve your capital.

Questionable Management Integrity

Sometimes, a management's integrity and its commitment to creation of shareholder value comes into question. A loss of confidence in a management's integrity is always a great reason to sell. However, don't expect the price to go down just because the management of a company does not have integrity. Sometimes, these companies will rocket up significantly before flaming out. The reason to sell when you question the integrity of a management is because you need to trust someone as the steward of your capital if you have to stay invested for the long term. Once doubts are created in your mind, every fall in price can seem like a reason to sell and it is difficult to continue holding the stock of a company which you doubt. Such situations warrant a sell also because investing in multibaggers requires conviction. If you lack conviction, you are likely to sell at the worst possible price. So, when management integrity becomes doubtful, it is a good idea to exit your investment and preserve your capital.

Selling to Harvest Gains

The other major reason to sell is to book profits. This is much more of an art than is selling to protect capital. In fact, the decision to sell is very easy in something that you doubt. But when a stock has been a spectacular performer in your portfolio, the decision to sell it can be quite wrenching. It is important to look beyond your own emotions in order to capture large profits.

However, it is very difficult to time your sell well and this instinct can only be honed through experience. This section outlines some signals to watch in order to make a selling decision.

Very High Market Capitalization in Relation to Market Size

Sometimes, a stock becomes so hot and expectations from it become so great that it becomes impossible for a company to deliver on such expectations. Usually this happens at bull market tops. When the market capitalization of a company is many times its market size, it is usually a great sell signal. Examples of this nature occur quite frequently. A great example is Zee Telefilms in the year 2000. The company had a market capitalization of ₹60,000 crore when the estimated size of the media business in India was only ₹10,000 crore. You had to believe that Zee would essentially grow the media industry by 6-fold all on its own in order to continue owning its shares. Once the bull market ended in 2000, Zee's price went into a free fall. The share price plummeted from ₹1,555 to ₹259 in about 11 months and has not been able to quite recover its old highs till the writing of this book.

Very High Valuations

The stock price of a company symbolizes the expectations of its future performance. This expectation is usually best reflected in a traditional valuation metric, such as the Price / Earnings ratio, or Price / Book Value Ratio, or Price / Sales ratio. When the ratios are very high, it implies that expectations of performance are extremely high. It is always best to buy when expectations are extraordinarily low and sell when expectations are extraordinarily high. High expectations mean that the stock price of the company can be irrevocably damaged if the company does not meet the exaggerated expectations. Moreover, a collapse in prices need not follow poor performance. Usually, when stocks are bid up sky high, there is a huge amount of speculation and momentum in the stock. A lot of people borrow money to invest. Once the price appreciation in the stock fails to keep up with the cost of servicing the interest on the money borrowed by the investors, speculators will sell to exit. An unwinding of speculative positions can completely damage a stock. Moreover, it is always better to sell multibaggers to speculators rather than to buy from them when there is a buying frenzy. Examples of sky-high valuations in recent times in India include Infosys in March 2000. The company traded at a P/E ratio of 343 at its peak and a P/S ratio of 100! This means the price factored in the earnings of the next 343 years. Visualsoft traded at a P/E of 277 at its peak. Zee Telefilms traded at a P/E of 757 at its peak. These were very unsustainable valuations. The expectations of growth at that price were absurd. These prices were impossible to sustain. All these companies corrected more than 70% from these highs and till the time of writing only Infosys could later recapture the high it had reached in 2000. The rest remained languishing near the lows they hit after the 2000 tech bubble burst.

> It is always best to buy when expectations are extraordinarily low and sell when expectations are extraordinarily high.

Though selling at absurd valuations seems easy in hindsight, it is never easy to achieve in practice. Infosys was expensive at a P/E of 100, but it more than tripled from there. If you had sold it too early, it is natural to have felt a twinge of pain and regret when it tripled. But it is always best to recognize that once a stock has given you a spectacular return, it is best to sell it and focus on finding the next multibagger rather than get caught up in analyzing how much more money you could have made had you stayed with the one that kept going up.

Vertical Uptrend in Stock's Price

When a stock trends up in a near vertical fashion, it is typically due for a massive correction. However, not all vertical uptrends will result in nearly permanent damage to the stock price. It is important to look for other signs of a top. A vertical uptrend combined with absurd valuations is usually a great time to exit a stock. It means that people are paying no attention to fundamentals and are only focused on momentum.

> A vertical uptrend combined with absurd valuations is usually a great time to exit a stock.

The buying frenzy in Indian utility stocks in 2007-2008 is a great example of this. A number of power utilities were trading at 5 to 10 times book value. Since profits of most of these companies were regulated by the government, these valuations were clearly unsustainable. But for a while in late 2007 these stocks just would not correct nor come down. Their vertical rise, followed

Figure 4.2: **The near-vertical rise and the following crash of the Utilities which touched absurdly high valuations**

---

by a collapse, is shown in Figure 4.2. But when they finally did crack in 2008, they fell spectacularly.

Over-ownership

Over-ownership of a stock is usually the reverse of the concept of unrecognized change. When everybody is talking about, or is excited about, a stock, it usually means that there is no value left in the stock because everyone has understood its underlying growth potential. High buzz around a stock, combined with high valuations and bouts of vertical price rise are usually a great sell signal. In addition to a general recognition that a certain stock will do well, a sign of over-ownership is high institutional ownership. Most institutions like mutual funds and hedge funds are peculiar creatures. They refuse to buy a stock when it is very attractively priced but rush to buy it once it gets well recognized. When a lot of institutions own a stock, it generally means that the potential of the stock is very well recognized. If you have discovered a stock early on in its recognition cycle, it is best to sell it into wide recognition. This over-ownership is also reflected in very high trading volumes and lack of skepticism about the company's growth prospects. Remember, excessive optimism is a great sell signal. The great example in this case is Reliance Natural Resources (RNRL). The stock went up 10-fold in a year from ₹22 in January 2007 to ₹224 in January 2008 (*see* Figure 4.3 on next page). A great majority of Indian retail investors were excited about this stock and held it in their portfolios. The volume traded per day rose from ₹1.97 crore to 1,020 crore. Expectedly, the stock corrected substantially thereafter.

> Over-ownership is also reflected in very high trading volumes and lack of skepticism about the company's growth prospects.

Opportunity Cost

One of the most important factors to look at when you are trying to find multibaggers is what additional return you can get from an existing investment. This is best illustrated by an example. Suppose you bought Infosys in 1993 and rode it all the way into the 2000 tech boom. By the time the stock reached a P/E of 100, it was extremely overvalued and there were several stocks in the market that traded at much cheaper valuations and therefore did not bear the burden of high expectations. Instead of trying to

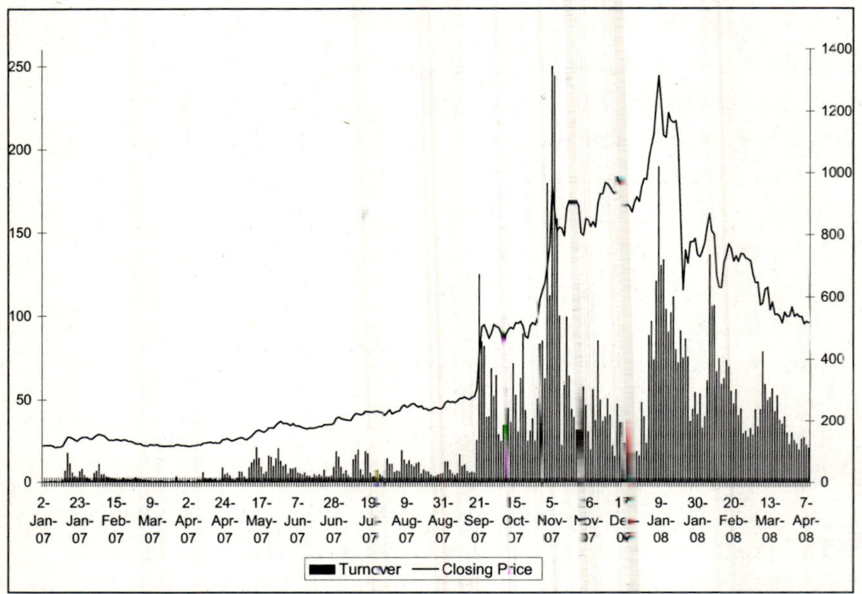

Figure 4.3: **When a stock exhibits over-ownership, it is usually a time to get out. RNRL in 2007-08 was a prime example of over-ownership**

---

catch the top, the prudent investor would have sold Infosys and bought something else that fit the criteria of a multibagger. Nevertheless, after Infosys hit a P/E of 100, it tripled once again. One might think of that as a cause for regret. But by buying a multibagger with a 30-time return potential, you would have done better than trying to catch the additional 200% return by staying in Infosys. So the basic idea here is that you should reckon the impact of opportunity cost in your sell decision. If you find an opportunity with multibagger potential and you own something that has already become a multibagger and is overvalued, it is better to sell the multibagger you own to buy the new potential multibagger you have identified.

Market Tops

A market top results in unsustainable valuations for some stocks. It also signals that some stocks will never see such prices again at a market top. So if you think a market is topping out, it is best to sell those parts of your portfolio that have given you dramatic appreciation and are trading at unsustainable valuations. What signs must you look for to spot a market top?

Firstly, look at the valuation of the index. If the index is trading at around or more than a 30 P/E, it is worth examining your portfolio to find overvalued stocks and getting rid of them. Secondly, if you find that there is unbridled optimism about investing in the stock market, it is probably a market top. If people you do not consider risk takers are starting to invest in equity, it is probably a market top. Also, a market top is created when the market goes vertically up. You should avoid buying at all costs during such times and seriously consider selling some of your holdings.

In summary, there are two broad reasons to sell your stocks:

- To protect your capital in case of non-performers, or
- To book profits in case of performers.

This chapter has outlined several ways in which to recognize non-performers. You need to understand each of these situations and develop your capability and judgement to distinguish between non-performers and performers. In the case of companies that have performed, you need to understand whether these have become overvalued to an extent that when a correction hits these stocks, they will not be able to recover. The signs to look for are very high P/E and P/S ratios, as well as high market capitalizations in relation to the external opportunity. Such situations usually occur when a market is topping out. Again, you will need experience to accurately judge when to sell in order to book profits. However, beware that every judgement will not be correct and you will need to treat every mistake as a learning opportunity rather than wring your hands in despair. One area of study that may help you in your exit decisions is technical analysis. Chapter 7 provides a very brief introduction to technical charts as they apply to multibaggers. If you see technical toppish signs combined with extreme overvaluation in a stock, an exit is probably in order. A deeper understanding of technical analysis may help you time your exits with greater precision and it is worth reading some good texts on technical analysis to develop your knowledge of chart patterns, volumes and overall market timing.

In sum, mastering the art of selling will make you a complete multibagger investor.

5

Understanding Bull and Bear Markets

It is helpful for any investor to understand the basic nature of bull and bear markets. Even though our research shows that holding good companies through bull and bear markets yields very satisfactory results, an investor who understands the nature of market swings can take advantage of very low prices to buy and very high prices to sell. However, be warned, no matter how deeply you study the market, you can never tell with precision whether it is in a bull market or a bear market, except in hindsight. However, it is worthwhile understanding these markets so that you can assess where in a market cycle you are at the time that you have to either make a purchase, sale or hold decision. In this chapter, we will outline some of the issues that can help you understand whether the market is likely to head significantly higher or significantly lower.

Secular Bull Markets

You may have heard the words secular and cyclical in reference to bull and bear markets. This secularity has nothing to do with religious beliefs. A secular bull market is an extended, multi-year bull market in which stock prices increase consistently. A secular bull market can occur in a stock, an entire stock market, commodity, bond, or real estate. It is usually characterized by improving economic performance of a country and good earnings growth of companies. There may be severe corrections from time to time within a secular bull market but since the overall fundamentals are not affected adversely, the uptrend continues.

Typically, a secular bull market occurs in three stages.

Bull markets are generally born in weak economies with interest rates hitting multi-year lows. The first stage of a secular bull market is characterized by skepticism and a total lack of interest in equities. Economic and company performance is lackluster or bad, and there is a general belief that things will not get better. Recall the gloom in 2003. When a market rally starts, people expect it to fizzle out quickly. When the performance of various companies shows improvement, scholars and analysts are quick to write it off as a one-off gain that will quickly disappear. In 2003, people believed that the market rally occurred only because of a good monsoon. In fact, *The Economist,* a magazine of some repute, was continually skeptical of the Indian market rally of 2003 because its writers believed that a bull market based on something as fickle as the monsoon was impossible to sustain. Large international brokerage houses thought that company performance had improved only because India had underinvested in capacity and a spike in demand sweated underutilized assets creating improved performance. Most of these brokerages expected that profit growth would not sustain into 2005.

An example in another asset class is the bull market in crude oil in 1999 which also began with the same skepticism. In fact, *The Economist* ran a cover story predicting "The End of Oil" just as the bull market in crude oil began!

Some other features of this incipient stage of a bull market are that equities usually form a very small percentage of household savings, the P/E ratios of stock market indices are very low (between 10 and 15) and small and mid-cap stocks trade at huge discounts to even tangible asset values. Public issues are not very common and those that do happen tend to offer their shares at very reasonable prices.

In the second stage of a secular bull market, there is gradual acceptance and wider participation in the market. Skeptics still abound but their vociferousness reduces. However, most people still continue to believe that the bull market will end shortly. The market, on the other hand, will defy gravity and keep rising. Those who like to sell short, sell the market short every time there is a correction and are forced to cover their shorts quickly since the market swiftly resumes its uptrend. The only approach that yields profits in this stage is "buy in dips". The fundamental upward trend in corporate profits continues in spite of skepticism about their sustainability. In April 2003, though the stock market had yet to display a clear trend, the CII Business Confidence Index for April-September 2003 was placed at 61.6 point. A score of above 50 indicates positive confidence while a score of above 75 indicates strong positive confidence.*

In the third phase of a bull market, there is euphoria. Everyone thinks the stock market is an easy way to make money. As an article in *Business Line* put it:

> ". . . making money in the stock market appears so easy that there has been an explosion in the population of day-traders.

---

* *Business Today,* 17 August 2003, Profits R Us.

> As a leading Mumbai stockbroker had explained to this correspondent, there are many such traders in Mumbai, Kolkata, Ahmedabad, Bangalore or Chennai, who come to brokerages armed with ₹20,000-30,000."*

There is also widespread belief that a new paradigm has arrived. For example, in the dot-com bull market, people claimed that business cycles were obsolete. The argument was that computerization had made it unnecessary to hold inventories or invest in any form of working capital, and productivity increases due to computers were so huge that we would no longer see business cycles. In this stage, people believe that the stock market can only go up and never come down. Valuations of companies become excessive. Several companies start trading at 50+ P/E ratios. Speculative ventures get aggressive valuations. Participation in the market widens dramatically. In late 2007, as the Indian market appeared to scale new highs, the number of demat accounts opened was 50% higher than the monthly average of the past four months. In addition, the total number of demat accounts with CDSL doubled from 15.55 lakh in January, 2007 to 28.24 lakh in November, 2007.** Most people ignore their day jobs and keep trading on stock tips while tracking the market on their computers. Retail investors think that the way to wealth is through speculation. There is widespread media coverage of the stock market and stories abound of people who have made millions by buying some company that appreciated spectacularly. The following news item illustrates this point:

> "Among the lakhs of devotees who flock to the famous Sai Baba Shirdi in Nashik, one of them stands out. K. V. Ramani has pledged to donate a whopping ₹68 crore to the temple

---

* *Business Line,* 02 November 2006, "13: and the Frowning Retail Investor".

** *Business Line,* 18 November 2007, "Market Book Triggers Rush For Demat A/cs".

> trust." The donor, Ramani, a software engineer from Chennai, made a killing on the stock market and says he owes it all to Sai Baba of Shirdi. He made about ₹200 crore in three years in stock market, with the Sensex boom.*

Another feature of the third and final phase of a bull market is that market indices rise vertically. Observe the Hang Seng index chart in Figure 5.1. Between August 1972 and February 1972, the Hang Seng index rose from 500 to 1,700. It subsequently retraced this entire move, and then some. Such vertical rises indicate that the market is near an interim top.

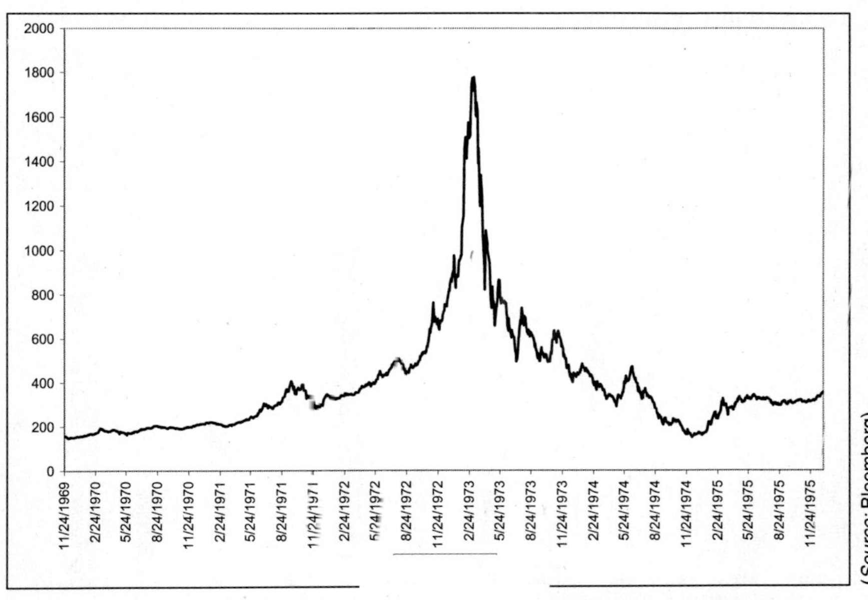

(*Source:* Bloomberg)

Figure 5.1: **In the final stage of a bull market, indices often rise almost vertically, as Hang Seng did in 1973, for example**

* http://saibabashirdivideos.blogspot.com.

To take advantage of this seemingly unstoppable vertical rise, a lot of investors start borrowing money to invest, believing that nothing can go wrong in the markets. Public issues are fast, furious and highly oversubscribed. As you can see from Figure 5.2, the recent history of IPOs in India illustrates this point.

Unfortunately, all this euphoria is a sign of the end of a bull market. Most individual investors end up developing faith in the market usually when there is no value left in stocks. They also tend to buy the lowest quality stocks. Also, by this time, leverage increases to very unhealthy levels in the market and a fall in prices forces liquidation of leveraged positions. Bear markets are born in this third stage of bull markets.

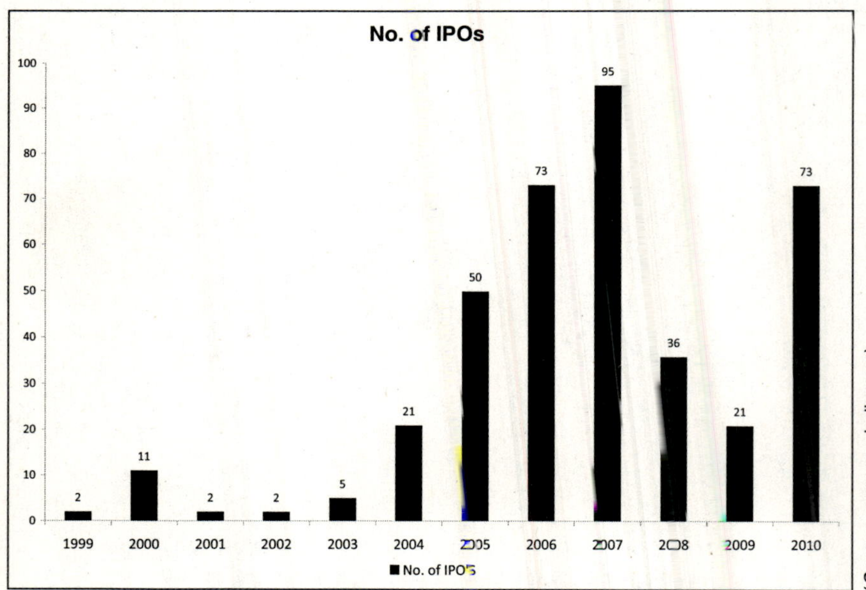

Figure 5.2: **IPOs increase in bull markets, peaking with market tops and then falling as the indices do. You can see how the number of IPOs changed from year to year in India.**

Within a secular bull market, it is possible to have several corrections. In fact, if you look at the history of the Indian market since the Sensex was started in 1979, it has risen from a value of 125 to 16,000 at the time of writing, an appreciation of 160 times (*see* Figure 5.3). This is nothing if not a secular bull market. However, during this spectacular growth spurt, the market has corrected by more than 30% on six occasions. In spite of these sharp corrections, the market continued to appreciate. These corrections can sometimes last several months, or even years. Such corrective phases are known as cyclical bear markets. These typically occur because of a temporary slowdown in earnings or overpricing of securities in the bull market. But once the earnings engine starts chugging again, the market picks up and continues its bullish trend.

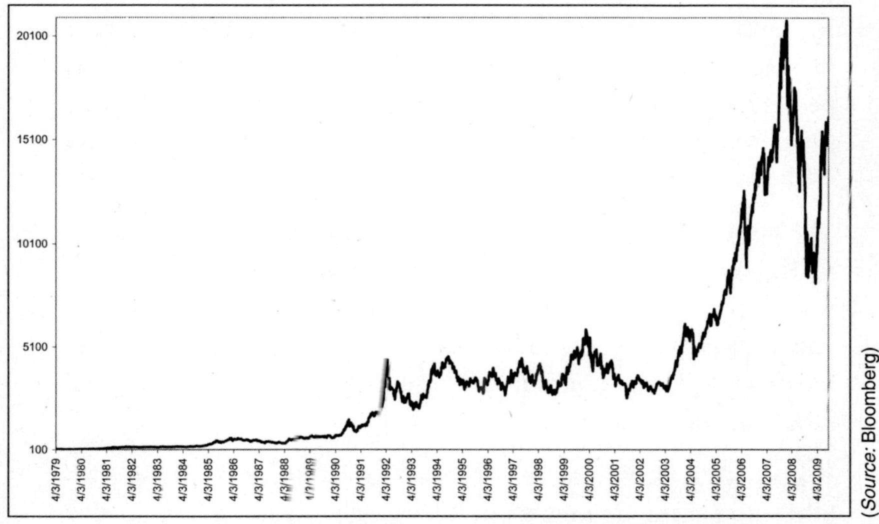

(*Source:* Bloomberg)

Figure 5.3: **The Sensex has been in a secular bull market since 1979, notwithstanding 6 cyclical bear phases (corrections) of more than 30%) till 2009**

A bull market can affect the fundamentals of corporate performance as well. Since equity prices rise, companies that need capital for expansion can raise funds without diluting their equity too much. As a result, their earnings per share show improvement. A multi-year bull market can actually re-inforce earnings growth quite significantly as companies raise cheaper and cheaper capital.

Secular Bear Markets

A secular bear market is a mirror image of a bull market. It is an extended, multi-year period of negative market movements. From the third stage of a bull market, a bear market starts to develop and share prices keep heading lower and lower. Bear markets are also characterized by sharp intermittent rallies followed by further selling. Japan is a great example of a secular bear market. In fact, it is difficult to find any other equity market experiencing a secular bear market at this time except Japan. The secular bear market in Japan began in the midst of the euphoria of the late 1980s.

The Nikkei 225 (*see* Figure 5.4) fell from nearly 40,000 in 1989 to 10,000 in 2008, a loss of 75% in the index. Individual Japanese stocks have lost between 50% and 80% of their market value. Every time people believe that a bottom has been made, the market plumbs a new depth. The market ignores all the good news and only focuses on the bad news.

Right before the first stage of a bear market, the economy is usually very strong, optimism oozes from every analyst, predictions of new, extraordinary highs in the market are rife, and interest rates reach multi-year highs. In the first stage of a bear market, there is complete disbelief that a bear market can even occur. As

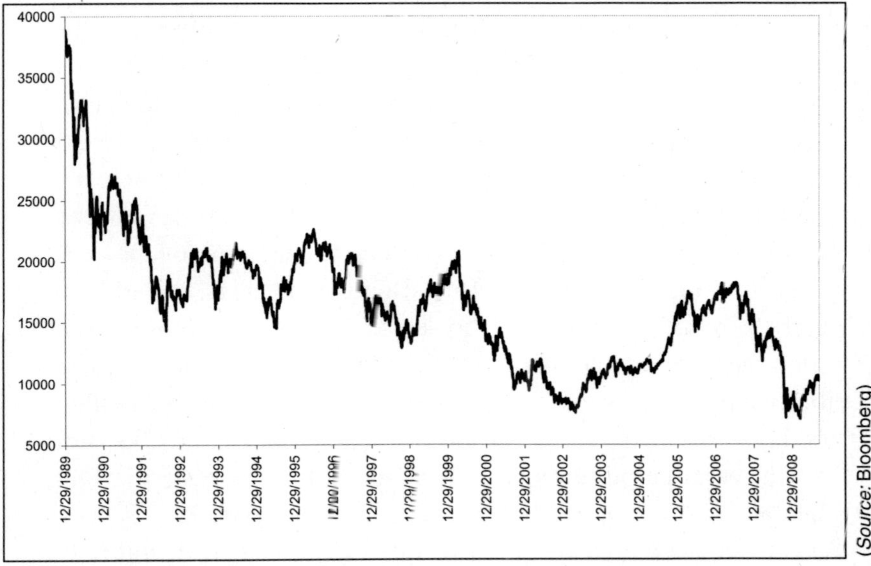

(*Source:* Bloomberg)

Figure 5.4: **The secular bear market in Japan since 1989**

---

prices start falling, leveraged positions are sold off to cover margin calls. This results in extreme price moves. But a lot of people are still in their bullish mind-frame and believe that a big dip in the market should be bought into. As people buy, the market rallies but typically they only provide exits for others who want to get out of the market.

In the second stage of a bear market, people are in shock. They cannot understand how the market, which showed so much promise just a little while earlier, can tank so badly. A lot of individual investors go into denial. In fact, they think that if they wait long enough the market will come back to its previous levels and they can at least exit their investments without a loss. But the market keeps going downwards.

In the final stage of a bear market, there is generally capitulation. There is a selling crescendo with huge volumes — and selling at any price. Those who had held on to their stocks earlier with the hope of selling at a higher price decide to get out at whatever price that they can get. There is total desperation. By the end of the third stage, investors will start finding companies at extremely reasonable valuations. A lot of companies will actually be trading at absurdly low valuations. Some companies will be available for market capitalizations below the value of the cash they hold on their balance sheets. Some companies will go into steep discounts below their book values. Low single digit P/E multiples become common. Usually this stage is followed by a bottoming out process where price falls do not occur but neither is there any buying interest from any side. As the market bottoms out, several corporate misdeeds come to light. Frauds that got hidden in the bull market excesses become apparent. Several companies will actually go bankrupt because of their inability to raise capital. This is the best time to buy stocks.

A bear market also affects fundamentals. Companies which require capital for growth cannot raise it easily. Even if they are able to, it is usually at prices which significantly dilute existing shareholders and puts pressure on earnings per share. This results in an EPS slowdown for the corporate sector as a whole.

Within bear markets, it is not uncommon to see cyclical bull markets. That is, sustained multi-month rallies that take prices higher — only to fizzle out. Among global equity markets, the Nikkei-225 index provides several examples of such cyclical bull markets within the larger secular bear market since 1990.

Consolidations

Markets do not only move in bull and bear markets. Sometimes they consolidate for long periods of time. In a consolidation, the index as a whole may not show any significant trend or movement. However, individual stocks could rise or fall depending on their own dynamics. A long period of consolidation occurred in India between 1992 and 2000 (*see* Figure 5.5). The Sensex, which traded at 4,000 in 1992, was still trading at that level in 1999. It managed to break 4,000 and go to 6,000 in the year 2000 only during the tech boom. However, this does not mean that individual stocks will not go up while the stock market indices are consolidating. Careful stock picking can result in exceptional

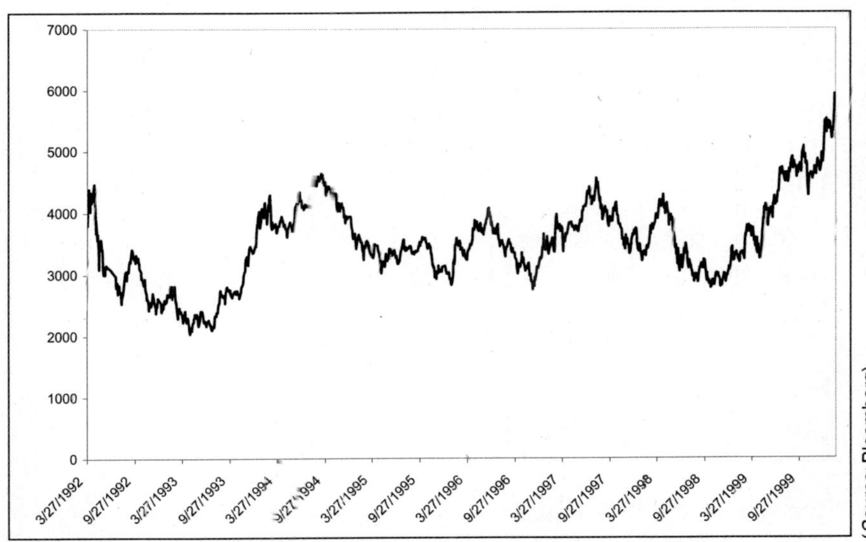

(*Source:* Bloomberg)

Figure 5.5: **Indian stock market was in a long period of consolidation between 1992 and 2000**

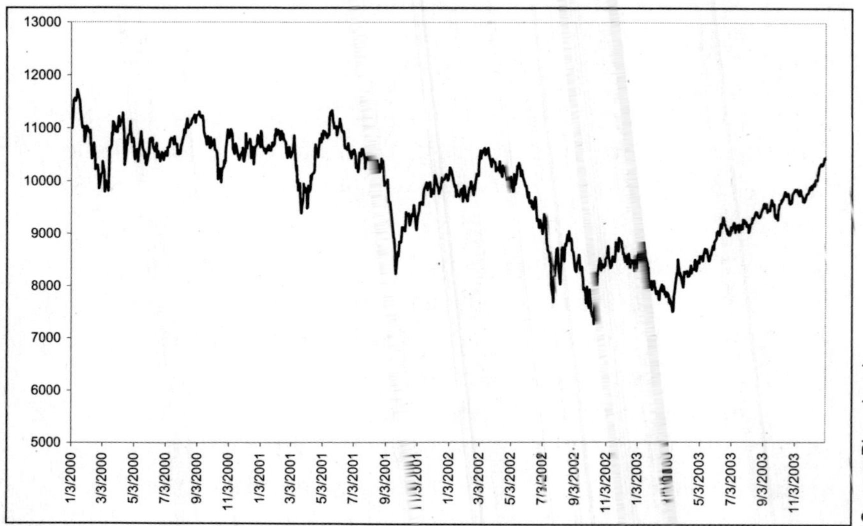

(*Source:* Bloomberg)

Figure 5.6: **The US Dow Jones Index consolidated between 2000 and 2003**

investment performance during such periods. In fact, stocks such as Hero Honda and Infosys became multibaggers during this long consolidation.

Similarly, the Dow Jones Industrial Average consolidated between 2000 and 2003 without much movement (*see* Figure 5.6). Consolidations can occur within a secular bull or bear market.

Why Bull and Bear Markets Occur

Equity bull markets typically occur because of several reasons. Firstly, there is cyclical improvement in most market-driven economies after periods of weakness. This is usually the result of several interest rate cuts and accommodative fiscal policies that are adopted during economic downturns. As the economy turns up and people begin to consume more, low interest rates encourage companies to borrow funds for increasing production. In addition, excess capacity that got built up in the past economic boom suddenly gets utilized. As a result, corporate performance improves significantly. As the equity market gets a whiff of improving corporate performance, it starts rising, resulting in a virtuous cycle of rising stock prices and improving earnings per share.

Rising stock prices result in improving earnings per share because companies can access capital markets without diluting too much equity. As long as they are able to maintain their return on equity, EPS rises when dilution is not low.

As a bull market progresses more and more speculative interest develops in the market. Typically, leveraged traders then enter the market, i.e. people who hope to buy and sell quickly. As the economic cycle moves forward, central banks raise interest rates to curb inflation. At some point, the interest rate becomes high enough to affect corporate performance. At the same time, the bull market pushes stock prices to unjustifiable levels. A high interest rate environment makes it necessary for equity prices to move up significantly in order to justify the cost of capital. When equity prices finally reach absurd levels and do not move up any higher, the leveraged traders start winding up their positions. As they sell, it forces other leveraged traders to also exit in order to fund margin calls. The market goes into an overall panic and various people are either forced to exit positions or are too scared to hold on to their positions. This is the reverse of the virtuous cycle of a bull market. Falling equity prices make it near impossible to raise money without significant equity dilution. This further reinforces the bearish sentiment and people sell until no one except committed holders of equities exist in the market. This is when a bottom is formed and the stage is set for another bull market.

The Effect of Market Cycles on Investors

In our research, we tried to calculate what happens to long term investors in bull and bear markets. Though this cannot be done with precision in the real world, we attempted to understand what happens to an investor who buys at every bottom in equity markets around the world. Similarly, we also simulated what happens to an investor who buys at every top in various equity markets. The results are quite surprising.

The methodology of our study was very simple. We looked at market tops and bottoms for various markets around the world. For the bottom fisher, we assumed that this investor would buy one rupee worth of the stock market index every time it bottomed out. For the momentum seeking investor, we assumed that he would buy one rupee worth of the stock market index at every market top. In neither case would an investor have lost money!

To understand this better, let's look at the Sensex charts from 1979 to 1992 (*see* Figure 5.7) and from 1993 to 2009 (*see* Figure 5.8). We have defined a high as a point after which there is a significant fall and a low as a point after which there is a significant rise. Points H1 through H14 are the highs on the Sensex and points L1 through L12 are the Sensex lows. A momentum investor is assumed to have bought one rupee worth of the index at all the highs. A bottom fisher is someone who bought one rupee of the index at all the low points. If both these investors had held their positions until 2008, the momentum investor would have earned ₹150 on an investment of ₹17 and the bottom fisher would have earned ₹140.72 on an investment of ₹16 (*see* Table 5.1).

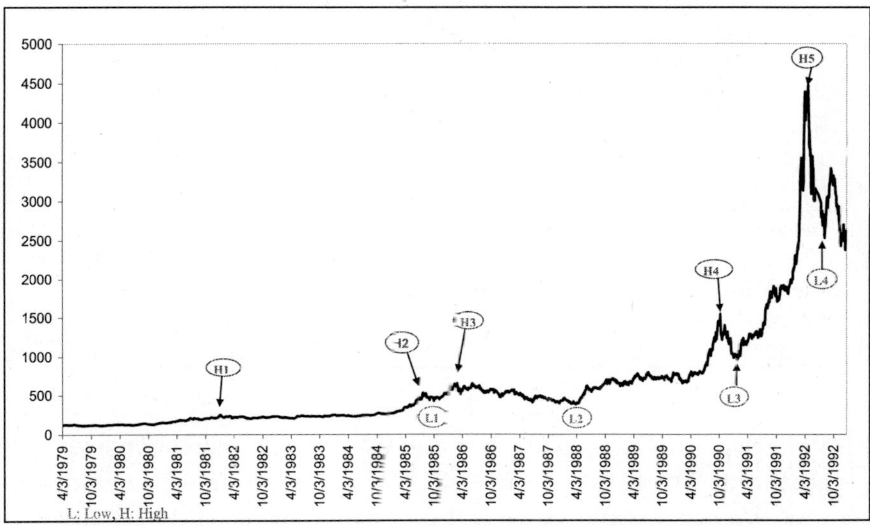

Figure 5.7: **The various Sensex highs and lows between 1979 and 1992**

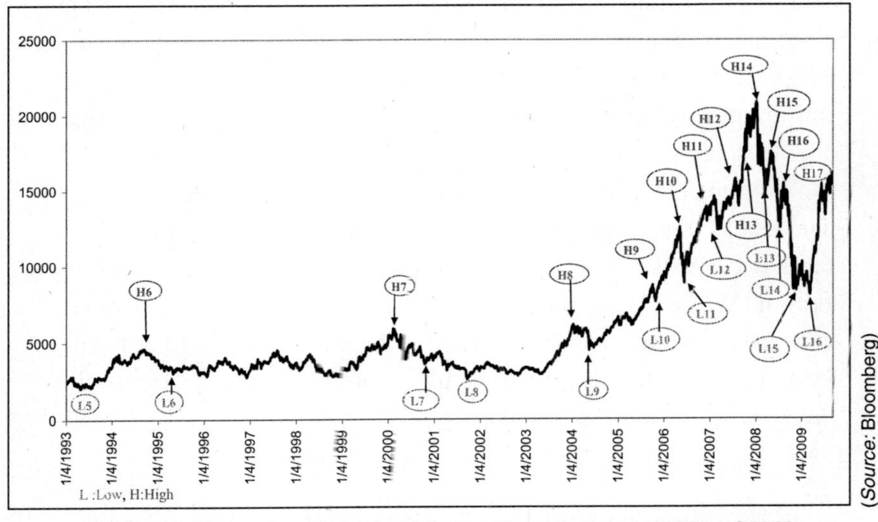

Figure 5.8: **The various Sensex highs and lows between 1993 and 2009**

Table 5.1

What Bottom Fishers and Momentum Investors Would Have Earned

Index	*Total Amount Invested at Lows (₹)*	*Current Value*	*Total Amount Invested at Highs (₹)*	*Current Value*
Sensex	16	140.72	17	150.85
Dow Jones	19	778.06	17	291.73
Hang Seng	18	300.16	24	178.75
Nikkei	19	23.35	26	29.29
FTSE	14	19.40	14	16.36

We made similar calculations for other stock market indices around the world (*see* Table 5.1). The results are quite instructive. We had actually expected that the momentum seeker would lose money, but he did not. This is buy-and-hold with a twist. If you buy and hold good companies for the long term, the timing of purchase does not have a material impact on the whether you make or lose money. However, you can significantly improve the amount of money you make by adding at market bottoms. The lesson from this exercise is simple: it is great if you can buy the bottoms but you'll still be okay even if you buy only the tops. The key is to stay invested for the long term. People with a short term perspective will sell great companies because the price is falling. While selling is sometimes merited, if you have a great company, the best way to capture outsized returns is to stay invested through market cycles until fundamental reasons for a sale develop.

6

The Relevance of Valuations

One of the most intriguing, almost mystical, aspects of investing is valuation. You will constantly hear people saying something is overvalued or that something else is undervalued. The most timid ones will say that something is fairly valued. What is valuation? How is something over- or under-valued? What impact does this have on the stock price? Without getting into the mathematics, I will attempt to explain the basic concepts of valuation and valuation's relevance to everyday investing decisions.

The core idea of equity valuation has actually been borrowed from bond valuation. Bonds are market traded debt instruments whose price depends on the interest rate offered by the bond periodically, investors' expectations of interest rates, and the time available until the bond matures. Since bonds make a regular payment called a coupon and a final payment of the face value of the bond is returned to the buyers on maturity, a complex branch of financial mathematics was developed to understand what the present value of all the future cash flows produced by the bond is. If the present value of all future cash flows from the bond is greater than the market price of the bond, it is considered undervalued while if the present value of future cash flows is less than the market price, it is considered overvalued. Aside from the coupon paid by the bond, the discount rate (or the interest rate) impacts the valuation of the bond. The higher the interest rate used, the lower the present value of future cash flows, and *vice versa*. This means that whenever interest rates go up or are expected to go up, bond prices fall. When interest rates fall or are expected to fall, bond prices rise.

This basic idea of arriving at the present value of future cash flows was then applied to equities. However, equities, unlike bonds, do not have fixed cash flows. This is because corporate profits which accrue to shareholders vary from year to year. In some years companies make more money while in other years they make less. So to smooth over this crucial difference, analysts began projecting future earnings streams using some average growth rate that they felt would be sustainable. Another crucial difference was that bonds mature whereas equities do not mature. So various professors of finance put their heads together and thought that a concept akin to the face value of the bond could be arrived at by saying that at some arbitrary point in the future, the earnings of companies would grow at a constant rate and that could be discounted to the present. This means that there were several totally arbitrary assumptions made in this valuation method:

1. The interest rate used for making the present value calculation;
2. The growth rate applied for each stage of growth; and
3. The terminal growth rate used to calculate the terminal value.

As a result of all these assumptions, this method of valuation actually becomes much more of an art and not much of a science. In reality, any valuation can be justified by tweaking assumptions of interest rate, growth rates of earnings, and the terminal growth rate. If you feel a stock price has run up too much, you can say it is overvalued by fiddling with your assumptions. If you still feel like buying the stock after it has run up dramatically, you can claim that the stock is undervalued by fiddling with your assumptions.

Though a lot of analyst reports calculate the fair value of an equity stock using the above described method, known as the discounted cash flow method (DCF), in practice people use different short-cuts to look at valuations. The most commonly used short-cut is the price-earnings multiple, or the P/E ratio. The P/E ratio is actually just a short-cut to arrive at the DCF valuation since the terminal value is actually just a variation on the one year forward P/E ratio. I will not get into the details of why, but it is important to understand this concept. Since the DCF assumes that there are well defined growth rates for the foreseeable future, and a predictable terminal value, of cash flows, both of which are very erroneous assumptions, the P/E ratio also makes these assumptions. So the P/E ratio is actually only valid for businesses with very predictable cash flows and a definable terminal value. This is not true of most businesses. A fair degree of importance is also attached to the P/E ratio of popular stock market indices. There is an aggregate earnings estimate that is arrived at for the stock market index and the index value is divided by this earnings estimate to arrive at the market P/E. This approach is fraught with even more dangers if you take it too seriously.

The P/E ratio is actually only valid for businesses with very predictable cash flows and a definable terminal value. This is not true of most businesses.

Another short-cut valuation method used most commonly for companies in the financial sector, such as banks, is the Price / Book Value ratio. Book value is essentially the value of the assets of the company that accrues to the shareholders.

A less common approach that I am recommending as a sanity check in this book is the Price / Sales ratio. It is very straightforward: the market capitalization of the stock divided by the company's sales of the previous year.

Peter Lynch, in his bestseller *One Up On Wall Street,* describes another short-cut that he uses: the Price Earnings to Growth (PEG) ratio. That is, he takes the P/E ratio of the company and divides it by the earnings growth rate of the company. He says that if this ratio is less than 1, it is usually a good enough buying opportunity for him. Since he was a practitioner and not an academic, his approach may have some more relevance to those who want to make money in the stock market rather than have an elegant formula to value stocks.

Having perfunctorily described these various valuation methods, I believe that most of them are irrelevant to the stock price performance of the company. Though analysts like to say that above a certain P/E or P/B a stock is overvalued, the stock may continue to perform brilliantly as the P/E or P/B can often go to absurdly high levels. In contrast, companies with moderate P/Es may never perform. Various valuation methods are very elegant in the way they are created and may have some relevance in corporate finance but rarely ever are they useful in generating stock market performance.

Then why is so much importance given to DCFs, P/E ratios and P/B ratios, you may ask. It is probably because a lot of brokerage analysts as well as institutional investors are still only a few years out of business school and they remember their lessons well. In most business schools, valuation is taught to be sacrosanct. The absolutely elegant way in which these valuation formulae were derived convinces a lot of people who have not experienced the rough and tumble of the market that valuation is a science and that all you have to do is to obey the law of buying undervalued securities and selling overvalued securities in order to generate investment out-performance.

Below is a little quote from the 2009 Berkshire Hathaway shareholders' meeting where Mr. Buffett, the world's most famous value investor was asked about the DCF method:

> Q: What type of discounted cash flow analysis do you use in valuing companies?
>
> A: Buffett: Investing is all about laying cash out now to get cash back in the future. The timing, certainty and amount of this are what you need to evaluate. A bird in the hand is worth two in the bush — Aesop said this in 400 B.C. and it is true today. If you need a spreadsheet or a calculator to get to an answer, you should probably pass. The number should scream at you from the paper. Munger: High and fancy math can be dangerous and lead you down the wrong roads.*

Clearly, Buffett is not a big fan of brokerage analysts' method of calculation valuations. The reason for Buffett's skepticism about a complex calculation is very simple: there are too many assumptions embedded in a big DCF calculation and if the fair value per share comes out a rupee more than the current market price, it is not a very clear buy signal. However, Mr. Buffett will also pay lip service to the idea of buying undervalued companies. Remember, undervaluation is in the eye of the beholder.

---

* *Source:* http://adamjdavis.com/tag/charlie-munger

Using the Valuation Short-cuts

For the purposes of this book, and in order to identify multibaggers, we will not even bother about the discounted cash flow method but rather stick to the short-cuts. So let's see how we can use these commonly used short-cuts which are reported daily in the financial media to our advantage.

Pay Attention to Extremes in P/E and P/B

These short-cut valuation metrics make sense only in the extremes, when they are either very high or very low. That is, there may be a potential buy when the P/E is less than 5 and the P/B is less than 0.5. Conversely, there may be a sell signal when the P/E is greater than 100 and the P/B is greater than 10. Values between these levels are not clear signals of anything. When the broader market is falling, even low PE stocks tend to fall, irrespective of valuation.

Use P/E and P/B Only as a Sanity Check

Just because you have valuations at either extreme does not mean that you can buy or sell blindly. You have to consider the qualitative aspects of the company as described in all the earlier chapters before you place a call to the broker. If a stock meets all your qualitative criteria, and it has a very low P/E, then it is probably a buying candidate.

Do Not Use Any One Valuation Method in Isolation

Suppose a stock meets all your qualitative criteria but its P/E ratio and P/B ratio are very high, should you not buy them? The answer is not very clear:

- You have to then check whether the P/E is very high because earnings are low that year for some reason and are likely to improve by next year. Another thing you should consider is the extrinsic valuation as defined in Chapter 2.

- If you have a company going through unrecognized change and its market capitalization is very low in comparison to the size of the opportunity but because of subdued current earnings its P/E ratio is high, you may still want to buy the stock or continue to hold the stock.
- Similarly, if the stock has reached a high level of recognition and extrinsic valuation but the P/E or P/B is very reasonable, it may still be worth exiting the stock.

Something that can often throw a potential investor off is a negative P/E. This is usually reported in the papers as a blank. When you glance through the stock quotations pages and see that several companies have blanks in the place where the P/E ratio should be, it means that they have negative earnings. How should the multibagger investor deal with such situations? It is very important to understand that even the best companies can have a few bad quarters. Various factors can result in bad performance during a certain year. However, if the prospects for the company continue to remain attractive, and the company has delivered attractive results in the past, and you do not doubt the integrity of the management, it is best to ignore the P/E when it is negative. If the company continues to meet all your qualitative criteria, has low extrinsic valuation and perhaps a P/S of less than 1, ignore the P/E ratio.

Another uncommon occurrence is an absurdly high P/E ratio. Sometimes in the initial stages of growth, even though the company is growing its sales fast, its profits may not be very high. This will result in P/E ratios as absurd as 500 or 10,000. These P/E ratios are meaningless and are not indicative of either overvaluation or undervaluation. Ignore them. If the company meets other criteria required for investment and is reasonably valued on a P/S basis and extrinsic value basis, you can either buy or continue to hold them in spite of absurdly high P/Es.

High P/E Ratio as a Sell Signal

The P/E ratio can be a sell signal under some circumstances. Firstly, you have to ascertain that the P/E ratio is genuinely high. Meaning, it is based on earnings that are substantial in comparison to revenues. So, a company having net margins of over 5% and steadily growing sales and profits may at some stage become very popular and get a very high P/E ratio. If this P/E ratio is very high, that is, it is over 60, and the company is extrinsically overvalued and prospects for the company's growth are diminished, it is best to exit.

Moderate P/E Ratio as a Sell Signal

Sometimes a stock that has appreciated greatly will enter into a stage where its growth starts moderating. In this phase, the company will have good net margins, that is above 5% of its sales, and its earnings and sales growth will remain steady at between 5% and 15%. The company's P/E ratio would have moved from very high levels during its phase of high growth to a very reasonable P/E ratio of between 10 and 20. Though this P/E looks very reasonable, when a company comes down from a very high P/E ratio to a moderate P/E ratio, and this is accompanied by a moderation in its sales and earnings growth along with high institutional ownership, it is typically time to get out of the stock. This is not because the stock is likely to fall dramatically but because it is less likely to appreciate dramatically and does not belong in a multibagger portfolio.

To summarize what I have said so far: the discounted cash flow method is very nice and elegant but does not result in a usable framework for stock market investments, P/E and P/B ratios are commonly used short-cuts but are only rough guides for investments and, finally, do not use any single valuation method in isolation without considering the context of the company's business and its prospects for making your buy, sell or hold call.

Let us now look at examples of multibaggers where the P/E ratio was not a determinant of whether the stock price would move up down or sideways (Figures 6.1 to 6.5). The examples being considered here are some of the best performing stocks in India.

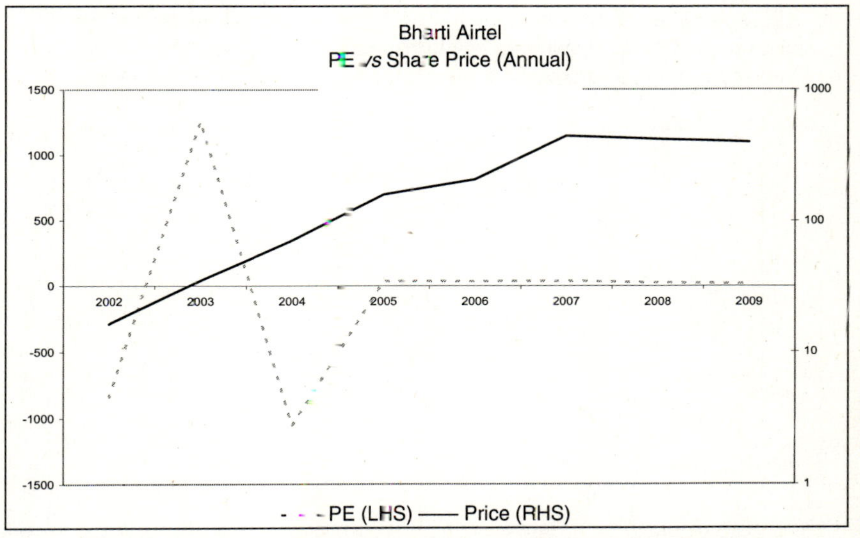

(*Source:* CMIE Prowess)

Figure 6.1: **P/E would have been of no help in taking a call in Bharti Airtel; irrespective of an absurd P/E, Bharti's share price kept on moving higher and higher**

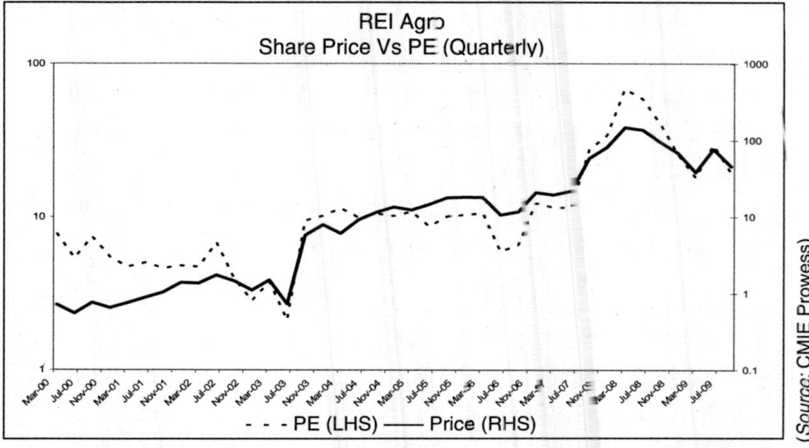

(*Source:* CMIE Prowess)

Figure 6.2: **Note how REI Agro share price moved higher and higher even as it was getting expensive in terms of P/E. The stock moved up in spite of negative earnings. However, once the P/E reached moderate levels, the stock also stopped moving up as dramatically. The bulk of the move occurred during periods when the stock traded at a very high P/E ratio.**

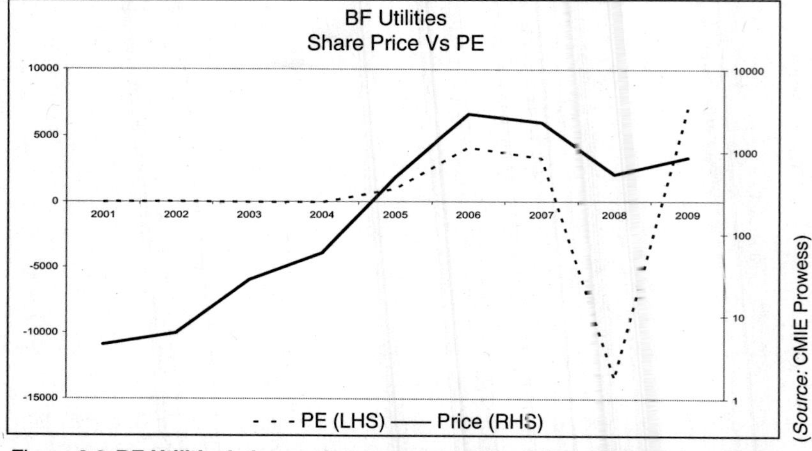

(*Source:* CMIE Prowess)

Figure 6.3: **BF Utilities' share price rose even though it had a negative P/E in the initial years. Granted, BF Utilities was a very difficult stock to understand given its very limited disclosures, but an investor who had full information on it but was depending on P/E to make a decision would have missed the entire ride.**

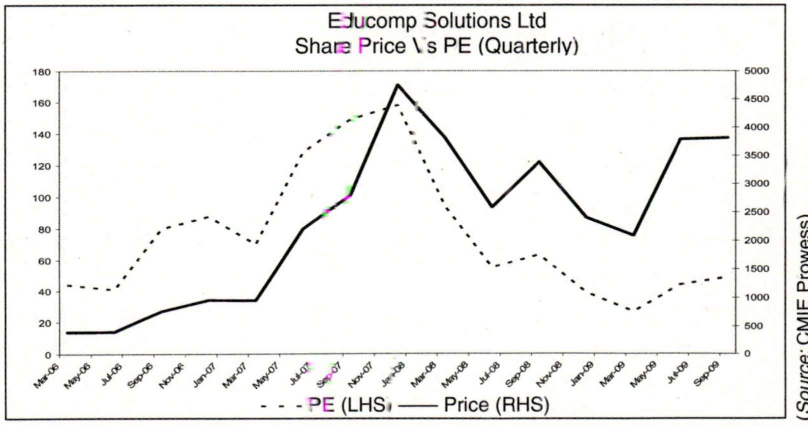

Figure 6.4: **Educomp Solutions was one of the best performing stocks of the 2003-2008 bull market. Its price rose even as its P/E kept going from high to ridiculously high. The P/E went down to reasonable levels during the bear market that followed in 2008-09. As the P/E retraced, so did the stock price. It remained to be seen if investors in Educomp will make a lot of money buying at these more reasonable P/E levels.**

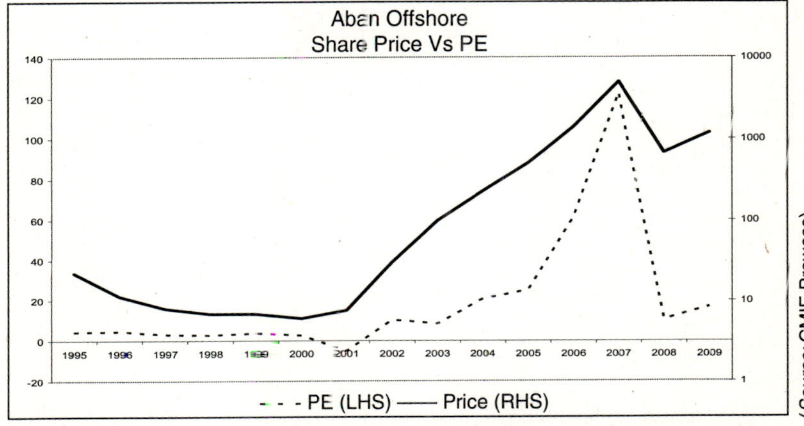

Figure 6.5: **Aban Offshore was another spectacular performer in the 2003-2008 bull market. However, a glance at the chart will show that the relationship between its price performance and P/E was tenuous at best. Aban's stock price fell as the P/E was falling and stared rising when the P/E actually turned negative! The stock price later rose along with the P/E to reach a seemingly absurd level of more than 100.**

To quickly summarize the point of this chapter:

- No single valuation metric is sacrosanct.
- Use P/Es, P/Bs in conjunction with common sense, market capitalization in relation to market opportunity and the market psychology.
- High P/Es can get to very high P/Es and the stock will keep rising through this period.
- The P/S ratio can be used as a sanity check when the P/E ratio is negative or does not give any information.

7

Multibaggers and Technical Charts

The much derided field of technical analysis has its loyal, and very successful, followers. The basic idea in technical analysis is that price movements contain information that is not available to fundamental investors and that price movements alone can be used to make decisions to buy sell or hold stocks. A lot of people feel that technical analysis is a pseudoscience which does not have any relevance to investors. Fundamentally oriented investors are especially skeptical of technical analysis. However, people who have participated in stock markets for long enough know that technical analysis may not work all the time but they understand that it works enough times for them not to write it off. A very detailed study of technical analysis is not within the scope of this book. But a basic understanding of the concepts of technical analysis can fine-tune decision making for the multibagger investor.

This chapter aims to cover chart patterns that an investor looking to generate multibagger returns can use to improve his performance. Readers who are very skeptical of technical analysis may want to skip this chapter and forgive the author for being so heretical.

At the very core of technical analysis is the historical price chart. Technical practitioners use a variety of charts, such as candlesticks, OHLC (open, high, low, closing) bars or point and figure charts based on their individual preferences. For the sake of simplicity, I am going to use line charts. The basic concepts that we are looking to highlight here do not require the details that are available in other forms of charts.

In this chapter, we will try to understand trends, support and resistance for a stock price, basic bottoming patterns, basic topping patterns and consolidations.

The very reason why a chart is used is to understand what a stock price is doing. The idea behind technical analysis is that there are trends in stock price movements, and if you can identify these trends early enough, you can ride them, make some money, and exit before the trend reverses. The ideal technical trade is to identify a bottom, buy a stock as it starts rising from that bottom, sell it when it reaches a resistance level, and in order to protect oneself, place a stop less below its support level. This way a technical analyst protects his downside, rides a trend and captures the upside.

Though it may be possible to use technical analysis as a timing device, it may not be possible to generate multibagger returns in one stock solely by following chart patterns. This has to be combined with all the other qualitative criteria that have been laid out earlier for buying, selling and holding stocks. A basic understanding of technical analysis, combined with the rest of the framework provided in this book, can be a potent combination for those who want to capture multibagger returns. Also note that several of the concepts covered over here are also covered in Chapter 5. The key difference between this chapter and that earlier one is that this focuses on improving entries and exits into multibagger stocks by using trading tactics whereas Chapter 5 focuses on market cycles and their characteristics.

Basic Characteristics of Trends

A trend is basically a strong directional move, either up or down. An uptrend is characterized by higher tops and higher bottoms. A downtrend is characterized by lower tops and lower bottoms. Both uptrends and downtrends may be interrupted by periods of consolidation, which will be described later in this chapter. Consolidations are not reversals. They are just interruptions in a trend which could either lead to a trend continuation or a trend reversal.

An uptrend may be reversed either by breaking a consolidation range on the downside, or after the formation of a top pattern, which is described later in this chapter.

A downtrend may be reversed either by breaking a consolidation range on the upside, or after the formation of a bottom pattern.

A schematic uptrend and downtrend with a top and consolidations are shown in Figure 7.1.

In the ideal situation, multibagger investing consists of buying the bottom of the downtrend and selling at the top of the uptrend. In the real world, this does not actually happen. Rather, we end up owning a stock during some part of the trend.

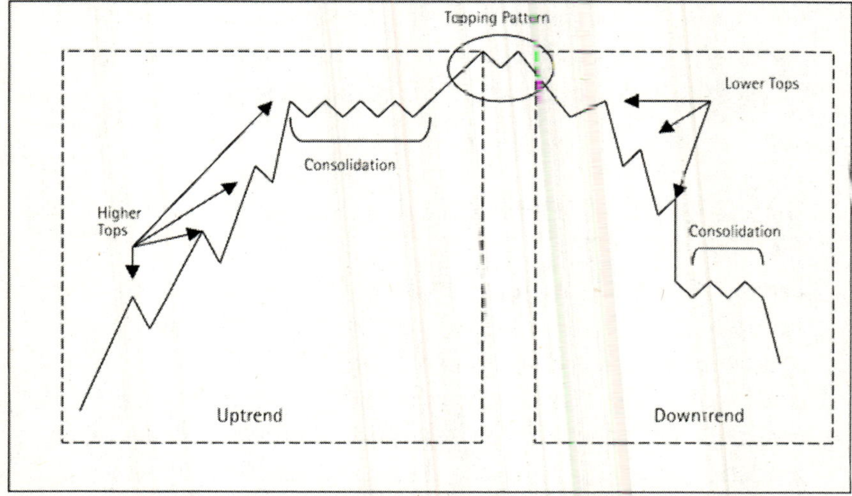

Figure 7.1: **An example of uptrend, downtrend, consolidation and a market top**

When to Buy

The ideal time to buy a stock is when it is beaten down and is just about to begin an upward move. In order to be able to identify this, we need to be able to identify bottoming patterns after a stock has fallen.

Another good point to buy is when a stock has run up, trades in a range, and then breaks out of the range. When a range is broken on the upside, it usually signals a further price up move. So we will look at basic bottom formations and consolidations in this section.

Bottom Formations

By their very definition, bottom formations occur when the market or a stock has fallen for some time. After this fall, a new rise generally occurs after the formation of a bottom. Recognizing bottoms allows investors to be prepared to make purchases when a stock begins to rise from this bottom. If the stocks you are looking at meet all the criteria for multibaggers that are laid out earlier in the book and are forming these various bottom patterns, it may be worth using a technical approach to buy them in order to catch them at attractive prices.

Double Bottoms

The double bottom is a simple bottom formation. Conceptually, a double bottom looks like Figure 7.2. The market hits a low at Bottom 1, rises to A, and then falls back again to Bottom 2. However, after making this second bottom, it bounces back sharply and starts moving up. Sometimes the double bottom pattern may be slightly different. Bottom 2 may not be exactly at the same level as Bottom 1 but may be slightly higher or slightly lower than Bottom 1.

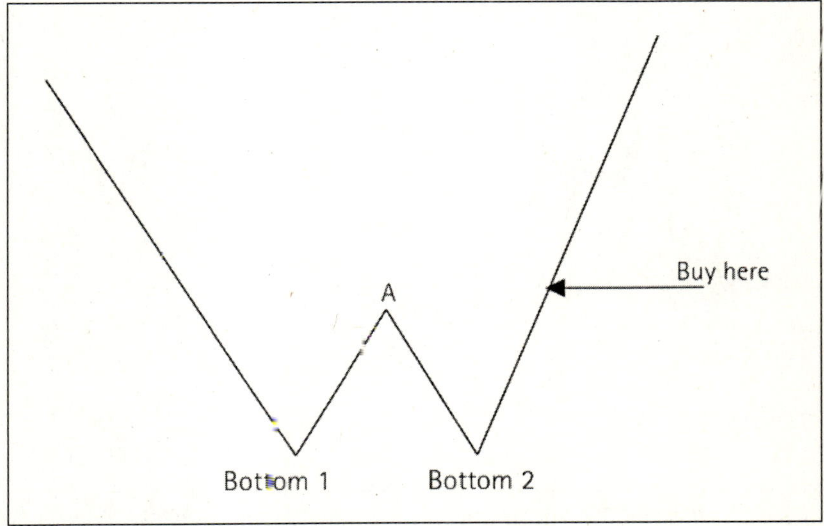

Figure 7.2: **A double bottom**

The right time to buy when you notice a double bottom pattern is after the reversal of price from Bottom 2 occurs and the price rises beyond point A.

If you want to protect yourself, you can also place a stop loss at Bottom 2.

The problem with stop losses is that they may kick you out of the trade sooner than you like but if you want to limit your downside, stop loss orders are one way to do it. Another problem with stop losses is created because of the circuit filter system used in the markets. You can place a stop loss, but because of circuit filters, the price may jump below your stop loss level. At other times, the stop loss will not be in the range allowed by circuit filters. So you will have to carry the stop loss mentally rather than having a stop order out in the market (*see also* Figure 7.3).

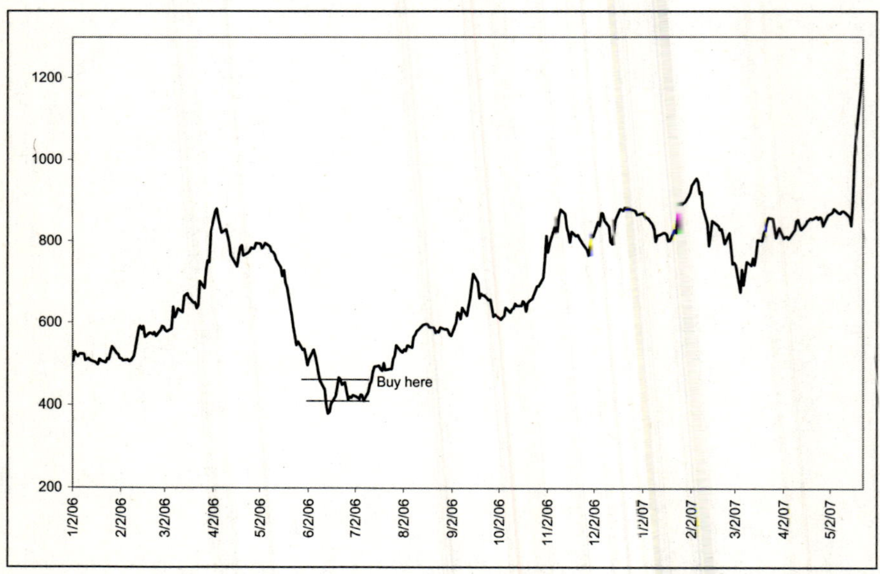

Figure 7.3: **A double bottom in the chart of United Spirits**

Triple Bottoms

A triple bottom starts out looking like a double bottom. It makes a low at Bottom 1 (*see* Figure 7.4), bounces to point A, falls back to create Bottom 2, rises again but either fails to go higher, or goes only marginally higher than A. The stock price then goes back to the bottom and starts rising again, creating Bottom 3. The line joining points A and B is generally called the neckline. If the stock price manages to go above the neckline, it means that a triple bottom is being formed. One should place a buy order once the neckline is breached on the upside with a stop loss at the level of Bottom 1. Sometimes the neckline is slanted either upwards or downwards. You may want to wait until the neckline is breached at the highest point before placing a buy order (*see also* Figure 7.5).

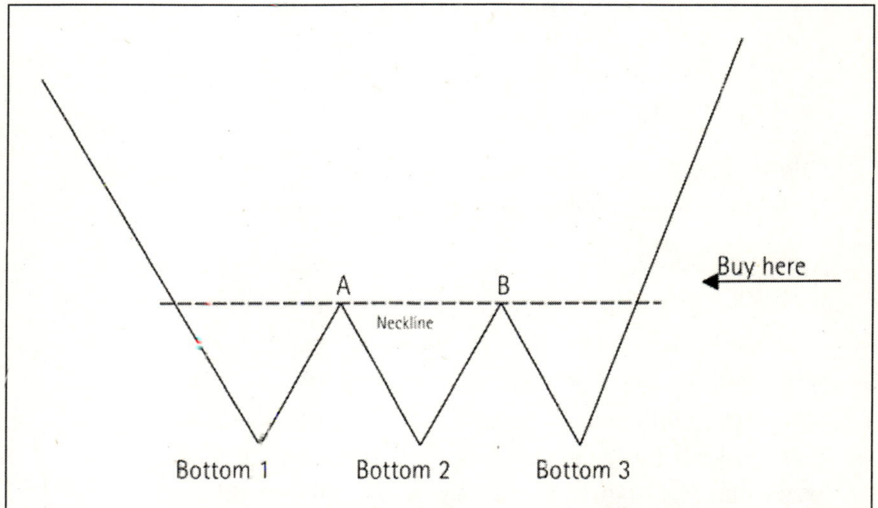

Figure 7.4: **A triple bottom**

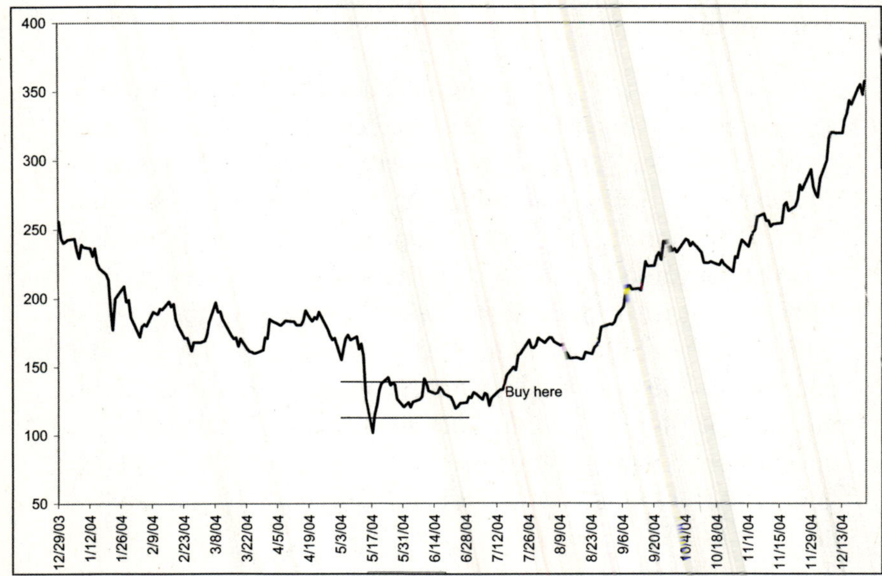

Figure 7.5: **A triple bottom in the chart of BEML**

Reverse Head and Shoulders

This is one of the more common bottom formations that occur. The pattern looks like the one depicted in Figure 7.6.

The stock falls to the level of shoulder 1 and bounces back dramatically. Just as people start getting excited about buying it, it makes a peak at point A, and heads dramatically lower to the Head. As investors start dumping the stock in despair, it suddenly heads up again to point B. It then drops again to Shoulder 2. In its final move, it reverses itself, breaches the neckline and heads up. The right time to buy is once the neckline has been breached on the upside. Remember, however, that the neckline can be slanted and making the purchase decision could be rendered difficult due to the confusing nature of this pattern (*see also* Figure 7.7).

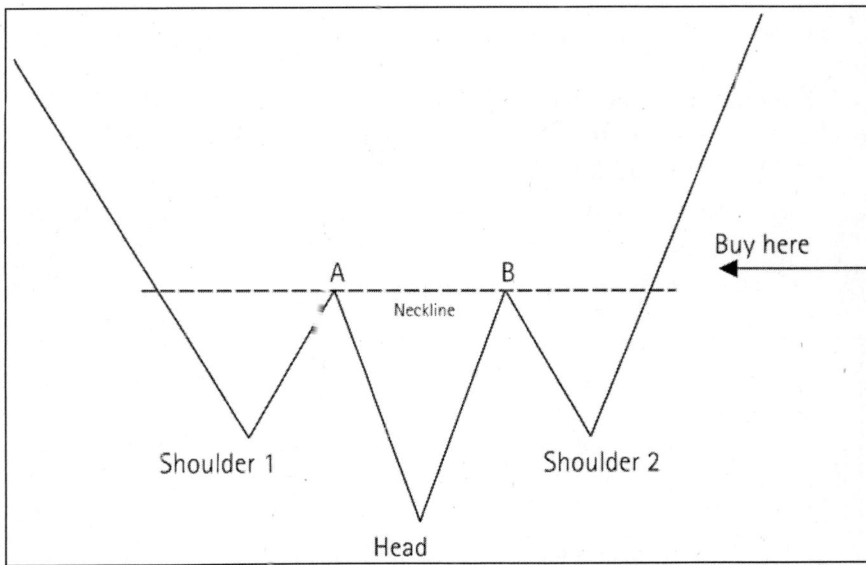

Figure 7.6: **The reverse head and shoulders pattern**

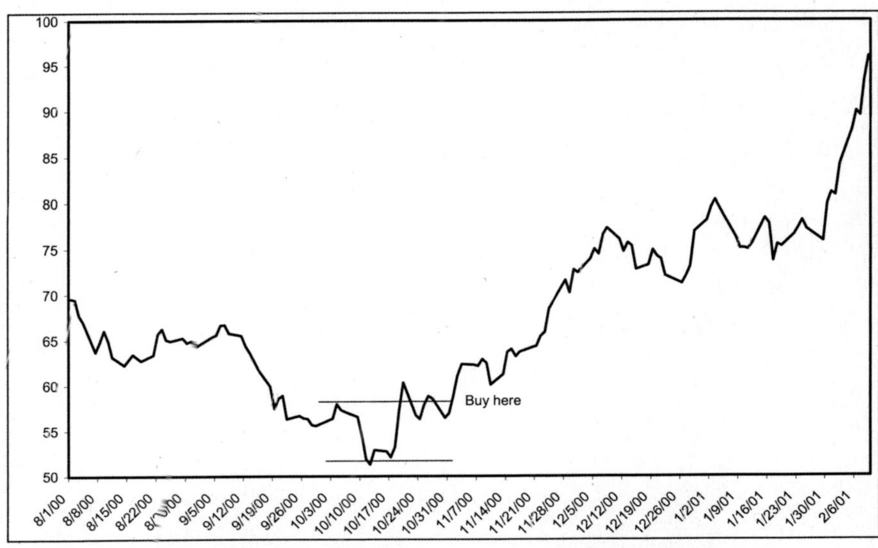

Figure 7.7: **A reverse head and shoulders formation in the chart of Tata Steel**

Consolidation Bottoms

Sometimes, a stock can fall from a higher level A and move about in a range between B and C (*see* Figure 7.8). Then it will suddenly break out of the range and start heading upwards. If the stock meets all the other criteria of being a multibagger, it may be worth buying it on the upward breakout at point E with a stop loss order at D (*see also* Figure 7.9).

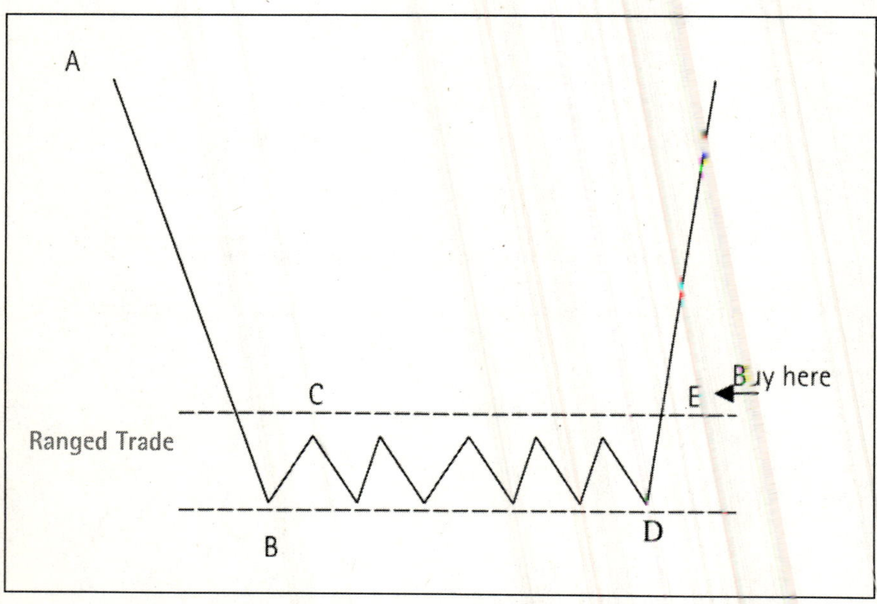

Figure 7.8: **Buy signal when the price breaks out from a range**

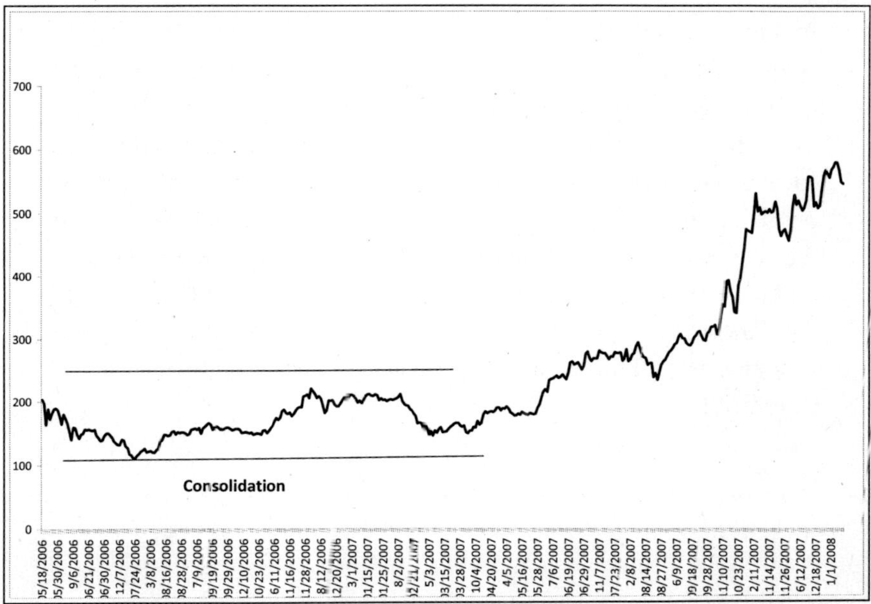

Figure 7.9: **Buy signal as Punj Lloyd's price breaks out from a range after a period of consolidation**

Cup and Handle

The Cup and Handle is a very powerful bottoming pattern that typically takes several months to establish itself. Trading the cup and handle is difficult until the pattern completes itself. A lot of people lose money trying to get in and out during this formation without waiting for the completion.

In the cup and handle pattern (*see* Figure 7.10), a stock falls sharply from point A to B. Then it trades in a very narrow range between B and C for several months before it suddenly begins a powerful move from point D to E. This is the cup part of the formation. Then the stock suddenly drops to point F and quickly begins a reversal move up. When it penetrates beyond point E on the way up, one should place a buy order with a stop loss at point F. This pattern is useful for someone who missed buying a consolidation breakout or those who did not believe that the stock was entering a bullish phase when it ran up from D to E (*see also* Figure 7.11).

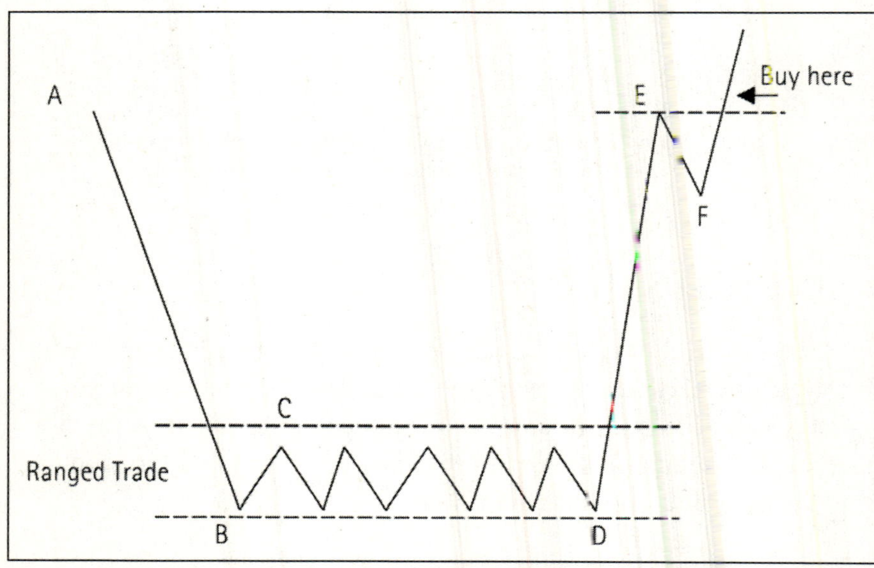

Figure 7.10: **A cup and handle pattern with buy signal indicated**

Figure 7.11: **A cup and handle pattern with buy signal in Dr. Reddy's Laboratories**

Consolidations

Consolidations tend to occur after significant moves either upwards or downwards. The nature of a consolidation is such that the stock tends to be stuck in a range without breaking in either direction. This is a state of affairs that can last for a long period of time. Buying during a consolidation can be extremely frustrating for most people. If a stock enters a consolidation phase after you have bought it at a lower level, it is very tempting to book profits. When it comes to multibaggers, for the extremely active investors, it may be possible to use consolidations to improve returns by moving to other potential multibaggers. But, beware, unless you are a very active investor, you may miss out when the stock begins its move again. Another important feature of consolidations is that they establish areas of support and resistance in the future. Figures 7.12, 7.13 and 7.14 illustrate what consolidations look like. The nature of consolidations is such that the consolidation range can be broken either on the upside or on the downside.

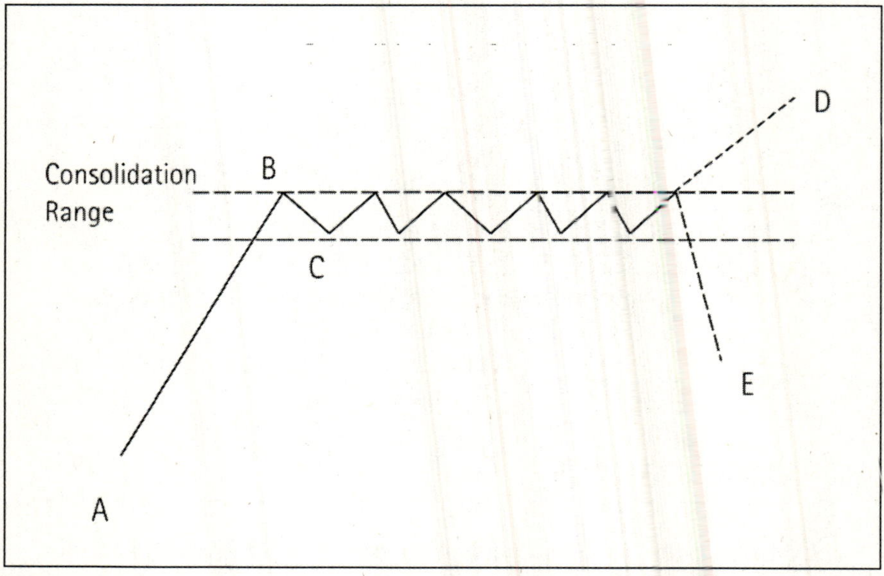

Figure 7.12: **Consolidation after a price rise. The price can either break upward from the range and head towards point D or break down and move towards point E.**

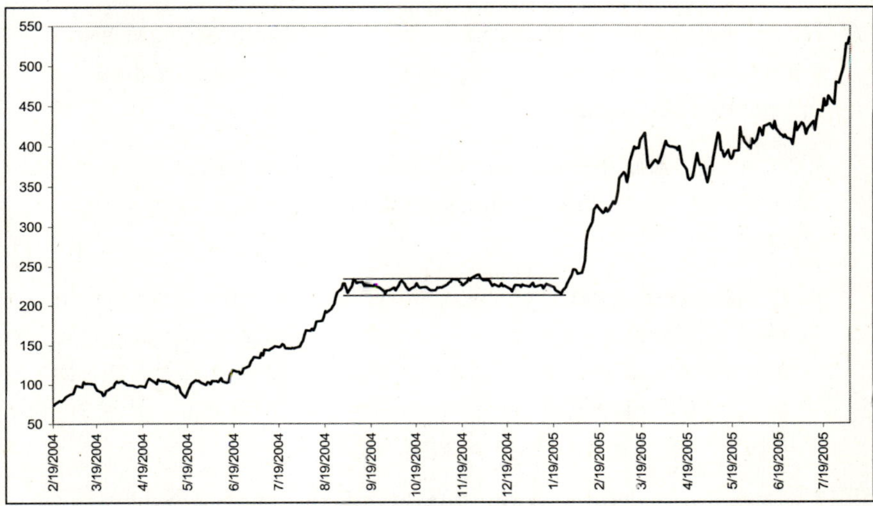

Figure 7.13: **The price of Aban Offshore resumed its upwards movement after consolidating between August 2004 and January 2005**

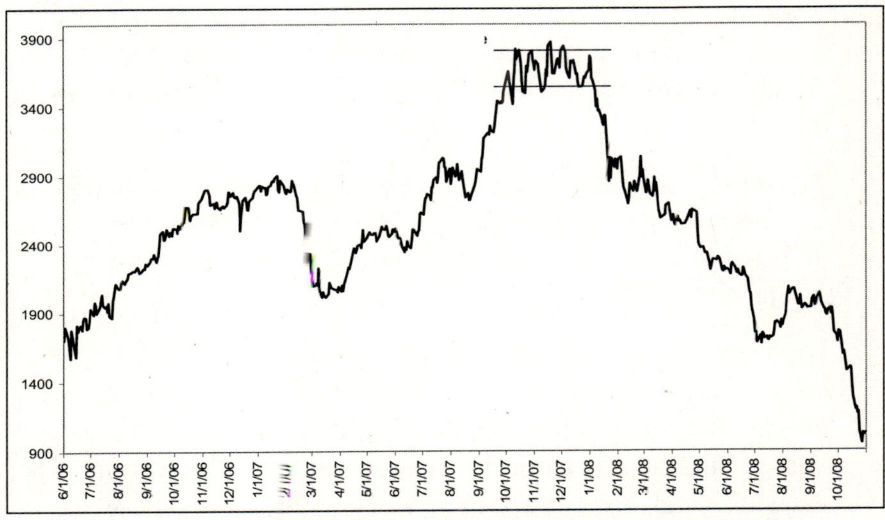

Figure 7.14: **After moving up from April 2007, the price of Grasim consolidated between October and December 2007 and then broke downward from the range**

Given these basic configurations of consolidations, there are a number of ways in which a multibagger investor can act depending on his circumstances.

First, let us look at what can be done if you bought the stock at a lower level and it has entered a consolidation after a run up in price:

- **Do Nothing:** Unless you are an extremely active investor, it may not make sense for you to do anything at all during a consolidation. Assuming the initial conditions that led you to purchase the stock are still intact, and you are not a highly active investor, this is the best option.
- **Set a Stop Loss below the Consolidation Range:** This will get you out of the stock if it breaks out downward from the consolidation range. The risk is that the stock may reverse and begin a powerful up move that takes it to a new high. In order to get back into the trade, you may want to buy the stock if it moves back up above the upper end of the consolidation range.
- **Add if the Price Crosses the Top End of the Consolidation Range:** If the consolidation is broken on the upside, it may make sense to add more to the position if you have the risk appetite and the liquidity.

If you are an investor who does not own a stock that fits the other qualitative criteria that are required for a potential multibagger, and it enters a consolidation after a run up in the price, you can use that as an upside break from the consolidation to enter the stock and set a stop loss below the lower end of the consolidation range.

What should an investor do if he holds a stock that has fallen in price and then entered a consolidation phase (*see* Figures 7.15, 7.16 and 7.17)?

- **Do Nothing:** If you prefer to be a passive investor rather than an active one and the stock continues to meet the qualitative and valuation criteria required to be potential multibagger, ignore the price fall. At some point of time the stock may rally again.

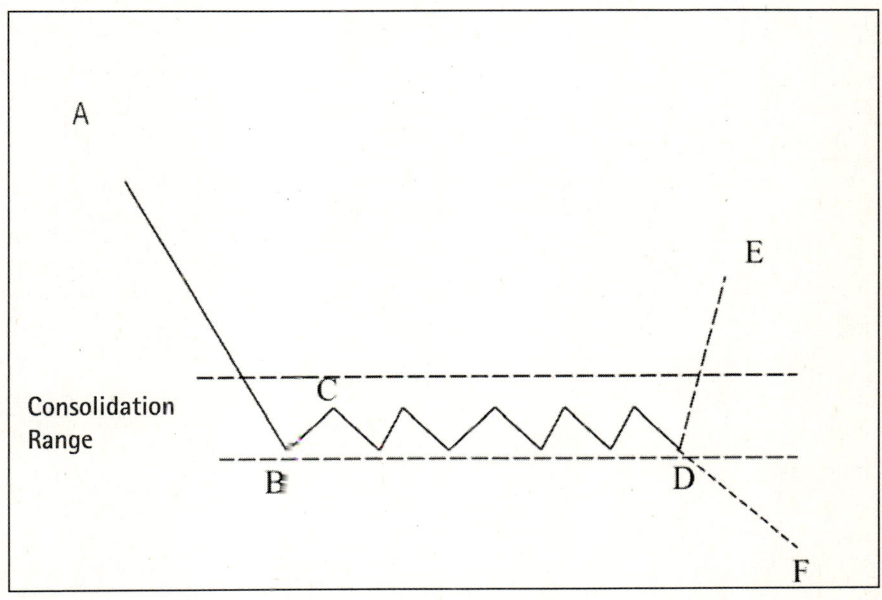

Figure 7.15: **Consolidation after a drop in price: a stock can either break the range to the upside and head towards point E or break it downwards and head towards point F**

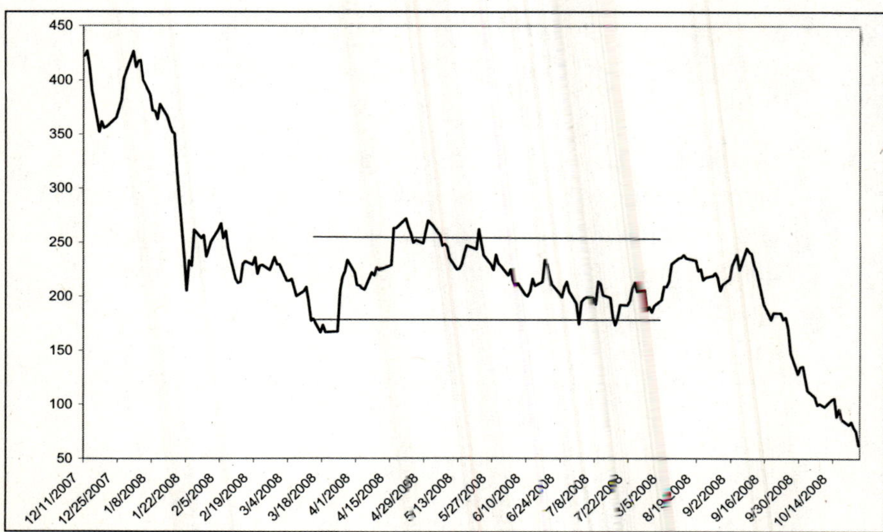

Figure 7.16: **The price of Aptech resumed its downward move after consolidating in a range for a few months**

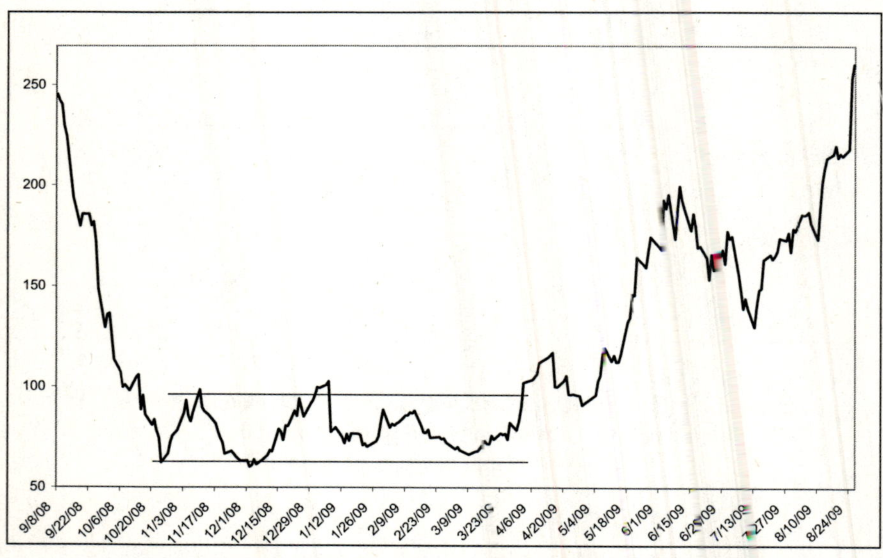

Figure 7.17: **Later, the price of Aptech reversed and headed upwards after a consolidation following a down move**

- **Set a Stop Loss Below the Bottom End of the Consolidation Range:** If you are willing to assume the stance of a more active investor, one risk mitigation step that you can take is to set a stop loss at the lower end of the consolidation range. So if the stock breaks the lower end and is about to go into a death spiral, you will automatically get out of your position. However, you may want to be prepared to re-enter the stock if it breaks the higher end of the range and begins to move up even after your stop loss kicks you out of the trade.

- **Add to the Position if the Stock Breaks the Higher End of the Range:** If the stock continues to meet the criteria of a multibagger and you have the risk appetite and the cash to buy, you may want to add to the position when the stock price goes above the higher end of the consolidation range. This will bring down your average cost and give you better returns if the stock moves significantly up. The key idea to remember here is to wait until the consolidation range is broken on the upside rather than to blindly buy every dip in the stock price.

What should you do if a potential multibagger stock which you do not own drops in price and enters a consolidation? The best option for you is probably to enter the stock if it breaks the upper end of the consolidation range. This may be the opportunity that you were looking for to enter the stock. Keep in mind that the stock should continue to display all the characteristics of a multibagger that have been outlined earlier in the book.

Support and Resistance

Support levels and resistance levels are often spoken of in relation to both individual stocks and market indices. The basic idea behind support is that there is a price level that a stock will fall to at which it will be attractive to investors. In theory, if you buy at a support level, your downside risk is limited because the probability that the price will breach the support level is low.

Support is determined by previous peaks, troughs and consolidations in a stock price. Sometimes, people like to draw trend lines and channels to establish support and resistance. Other people use more complex mathematical calculations known as Fibonacci numbers and Gann lines to establish support and resistance levels. All these methods work some of the time. Here I will illustrate the simplest method of identifying a support level that is suitable for long term investors rather than active traders.

If a stock that was moving up consolidates at a particular level on the way down, the top of that consolidation is often thought of as support. Figure 7.18 demonstrates this concept. Similarly, previous peaks in the stock price are also thought of as support.

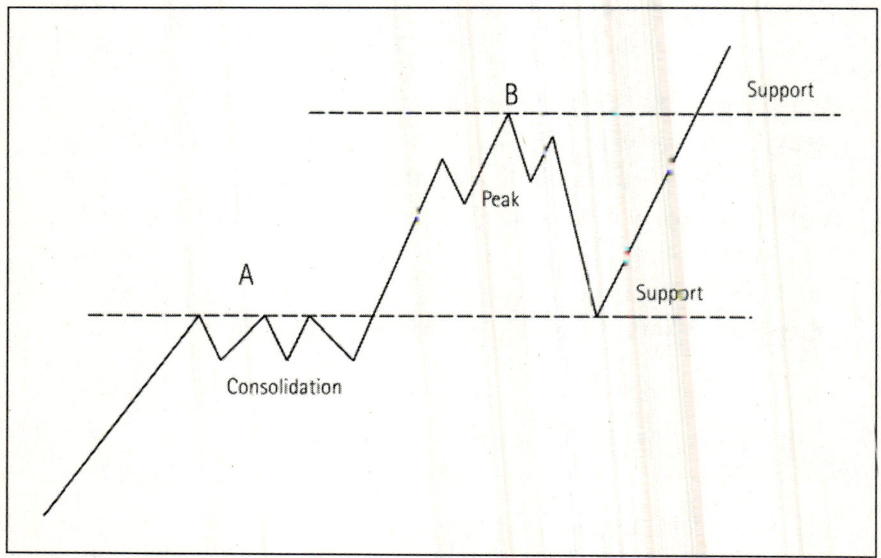

Figure 7.18: **Support and resistance areas**

In Figure 7.18, the stock rises to point A and consolidates for some time. Once the stock breaks out and moves higher to point B, it peaks. When the stock falls from the peak level B, point A acts as support and the stock bounces from this support level. Similarly, after the stock breaks above the peak established at point B, B becomes a new support level.

Remember, however, that a support is not sacrosanct. It can be broken on the downside as well. The stock need not have bounced from the support level created at the consolidation level A. It could have breached the support level and headed down significantly. So a lot of people buy stocks when they bounce from the support level and place a stop loss right below the support level so that their downside is protected (*see also* Figure 7.19).

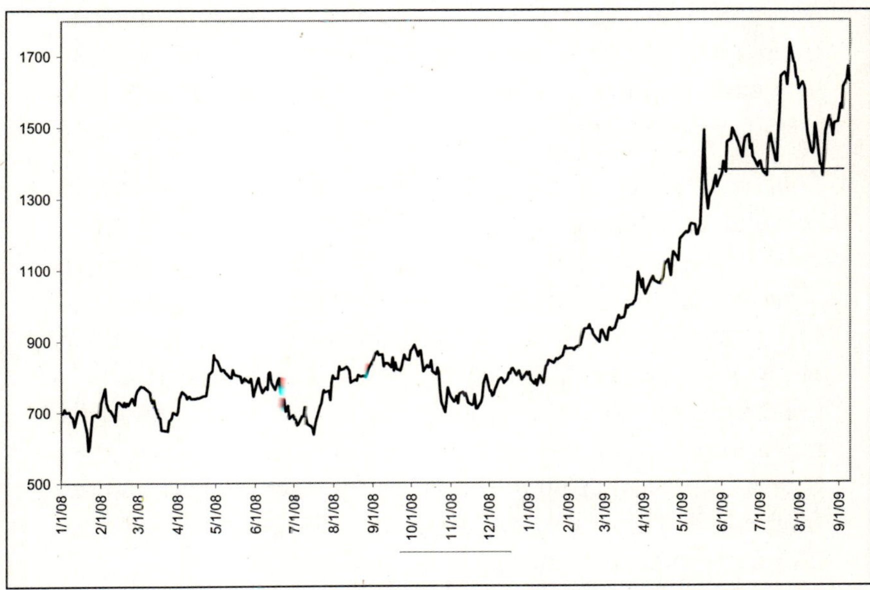

Figure 7.19: **A classic support pattern in the chart of Hero Honda**

How does a support level help a multibagger investor? Suppose you believe that a particular stock has multibagger potential and has all the other characteristics that have been outlined earlier in the book. Now, suppose this stock starts dropping. It is not the best idea to jump in and buy as soon as a stock begins to drop. You will want to wait until it reaches a support level and begins bouncing from there. Buy the bounce from the support level and place a stop loss a few points below the support level. This way, if the stock truly bounces from the support level, you will get the stock at a very attractive price and your downside is protected because you have placed a stop loss order below the support level.

Having covered support, let us move on to resistance levels.

Resistance is very similar to the support concept. It is determined using previous peaks, troughs, trend lines, Fibonacci numbers, Gann lines, and what have you. I am going to cover only the very basic notion of resistance and how it is derived, which is on previous consolidations, peaks and troughs.

Look at the diagram in Figure 7.20. The stock is on its way up, consolidates at point A, establishes a support level, moves to peak B and reverses into a downtrend. Then technical analysis suggests that the lower end of the toppish pattern at peak is the first resistance to any short term uptrend within the downtrend. So, as the stock falls, it suddenly develops an intermediate up-trend from point C. This uptrend reaches the lower end of the range formed while the stock price peaked. From D, the stock begins its descent again to E. There is another pullback in price from E to F. Then the stock falls again to G, at which point it has broken the support created by consolidation at point A.

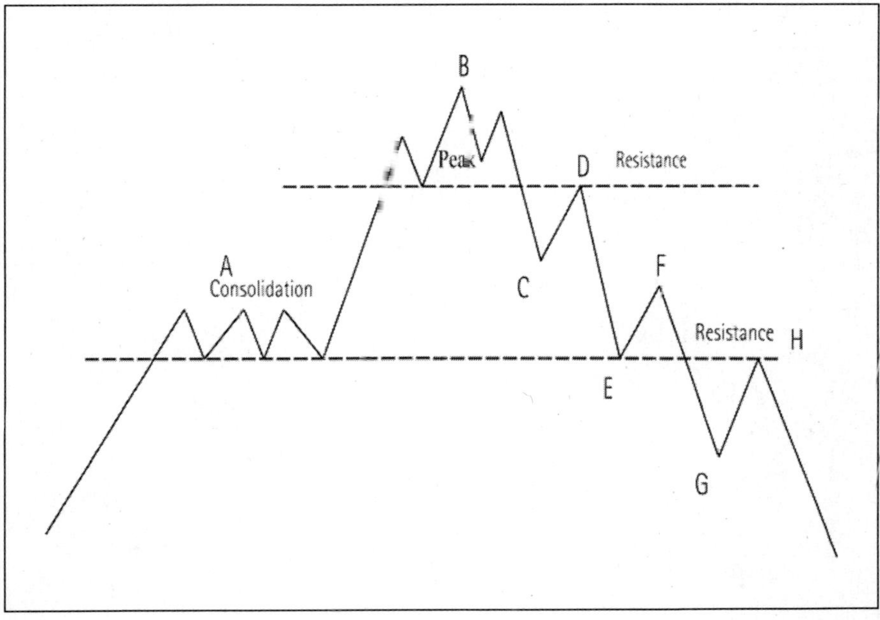

Figure 7.20: **On its way up, the stock consolidates at point A, establishing a support level, moves to peak B and reverses into a downtrend and find support at E. There is another pullback in price from E to F. Then the stock falls again to G, at which point it has broken the support created by consolidation at point A. A key thing to remember is that after a support has been broken, it becomes resistance, and *vice versa*. So the support level that was broken at E is now resistance for every attempt at an up move.**

(Continued . . .)

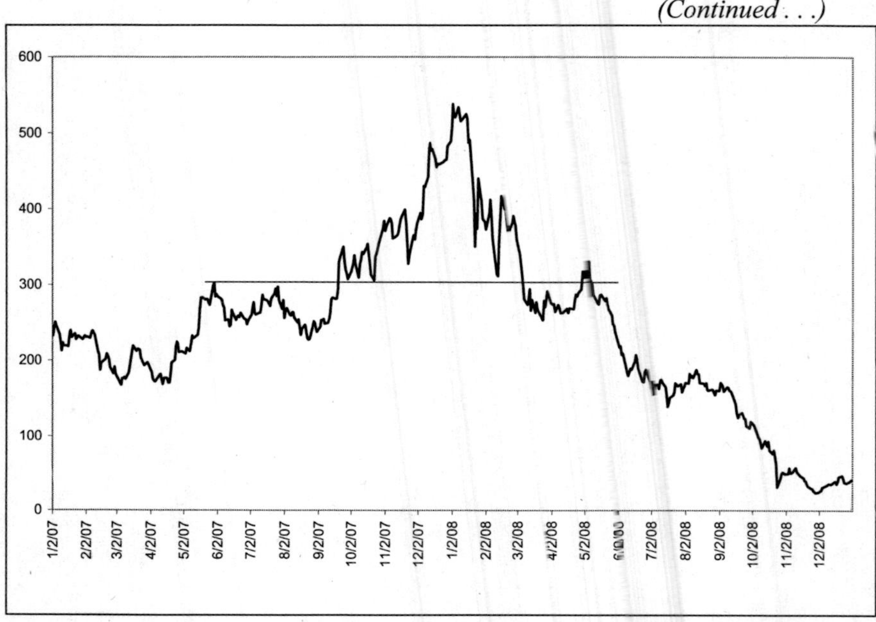

Figure 7.21: **The classic phenomenon of support becoming resistance in the chart of Unitech**

A key thing to remember is that after a support has been broken, it becomes resistance, and *vice versa.* So the support level that was broken at E is now resistance for every attempt at an up move. As illustrated in the diagram, the stock makes an attempt to move up from G but meets resistance at H, which was a support level before and then recommences its descent (*see also* Figure 7.21).

If you are a multibagger investor, you can use the concept of resistance to your advantage. Suppose you already own a stock which peaked at point A and then started falling. Also, assume that the stock is overvalued both on a P/E basis and an extrinsic valuation basis but you have been holding on because the stock has stubbornly moved up. Once the stock falls below the neckline of the peak and begins its up move, it is easy to believe that the uptrend has resumed. But knowing that there is resistance at point D gives you a well defined exit point. If the stock price fails to move past point D, you can book profits and get out of the stock without waiting for further erosion in its value. However, if you do not believe that it is overvalued, it may not be the best idea to get out after it fails to cross D, unless you want to keep trading in and out of the stock as it reaches its full potential. In case you want to trade back into the stock, you may want to buy if the stock price convincingly goes past point D.

Suppose do not own the stock. The consolidation support level that was formed at point A is a very strong one. By knowing that the stock could bounce strongly and move up from there, you could wait to buy if it breached the higher end of the consolidation range formed at point A. If it does, you can buy immediately. But if it does not, even though the valuation may be attractive and the company may have very good prospects, and instead breaches the support level at that consolidation and heads towards point G, you should not buy until the stock goes above the resistance level at H unless you are prepared to suffer more downside.

Tops

The ability to recognize tops can help you get out of situations that can erode tremendous wealth. It may be a good idea to use top patterns as a confirmation of your own estimate of overvaluation of a company.

It may be a good idea to use top patterns as a confirmation of your own estimate of overvaluation of a company.

It is generally difficult to get a multibagger return if you panic at every top and sell out. That makes you more of a trader than an investor. That is not to say that trading is bad but you may incur a lot of transaction costs as well as having to pay more in taxes if you keep trading in and out of a stock. Also, chances are that you will not be able to capture the entire multibagger return if you are constantly darting in and out of the stock. However, if you believe that a stock is overvalued both on traditional valuation levels as well as on extrinsic valuation, it has already given you a multibagger return and you believe that the entire market is over-exuberant, selling at a top may be a wise decision.

Double Top

A double top is a classic pattern. The stock price makes a new high but falls from it. It then runs back up to the high but fails to cross that level and starts falling on high volumes. The pattern is shown in Figure 7.22.

Double tops, like double bottoms, can be irregular. This means that a test of the first top may occur at a slightly higher, or slightly lower, level. The valley level of the double top defines what is known as a neckline. A breach on the neckline is typically considered to be confirmation that a trend reversal has occurred. So a multibagger investor who owns a stock that he believes is overvalued should exit if the stock breaches the neckline of a double top. Sometimes what looks like a double top may only end up being a consolidation. So it is important to let the neckline be breached before any action is taken (*see also* Figure 7.23).

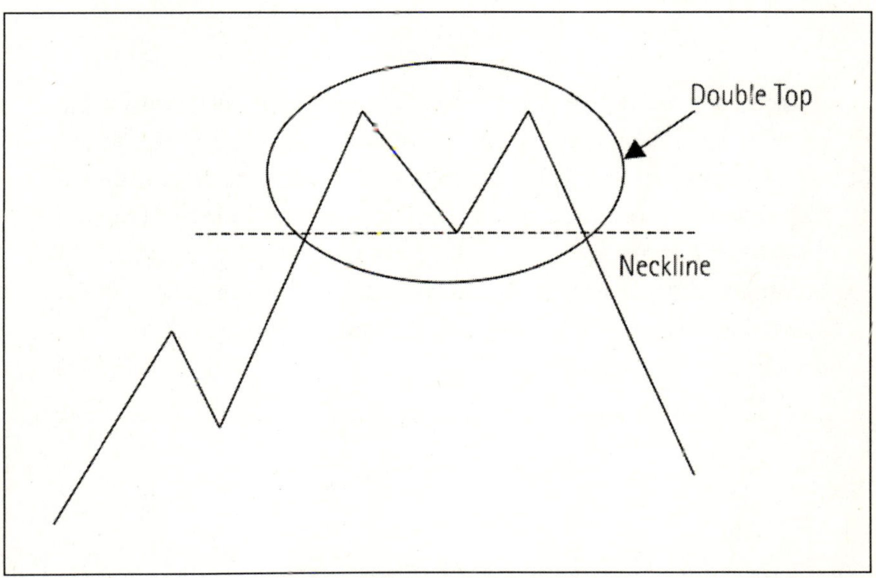

Figure 7.22: **Double top formation**

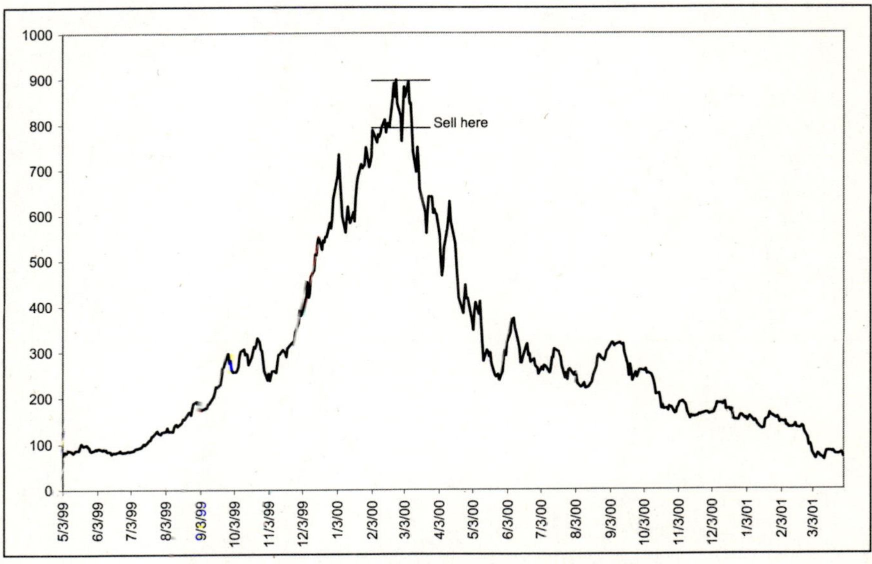

Figure 7.23: **A double top in the chart of Zee**

Triple Top

A triple top is another top formation which is a variation on the double top. In this case, what looks like a double top is formed but the neckline is not breached. Instead, the stock tries to retest the high one more time but fails. The neckline is then breached and the stock reverses trend and falls dramatically. Figure 7.24 illustrates a triple top. In this case, too, an investor who holds a stock that he believes is overvalued should sell on a breach of the neckline (*see also* Figure 7.25).

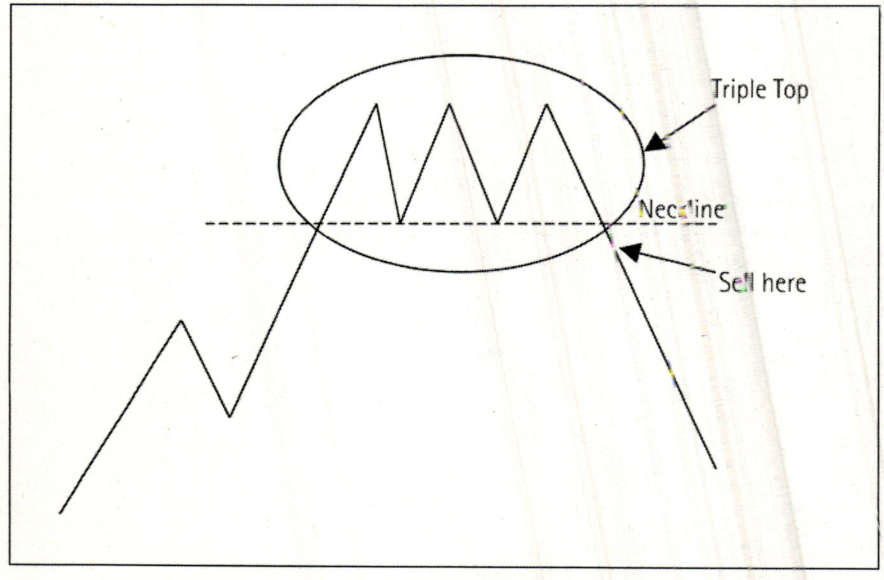

Figure 7.24: **A triple top**

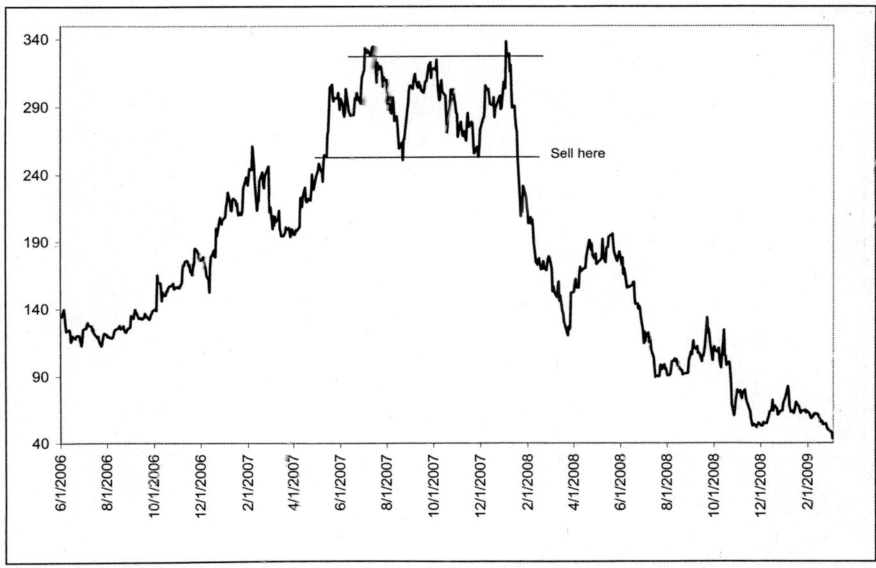

Figure 7.25: **A triple top in the price chart of Moser Baer**

Head and Shoulders

A head and shoulders pattern (Figure 7.26) is a highly confusing top pattern that fools a lot of investors. The stock will behave as though it is actually in an uptrend by making a higher high. Immediately after making a higher high it will suddenly make a lower high instead of a higher high. This pattern takes several days, and sometimes weeks, to play itself out and kills a lot of traders as it forms because it is so confusing. Training yourself to recognize head and shoulder patterns will give you a great exit point. This pattern can only be recognized once the stock fails to make a new high but not before that.

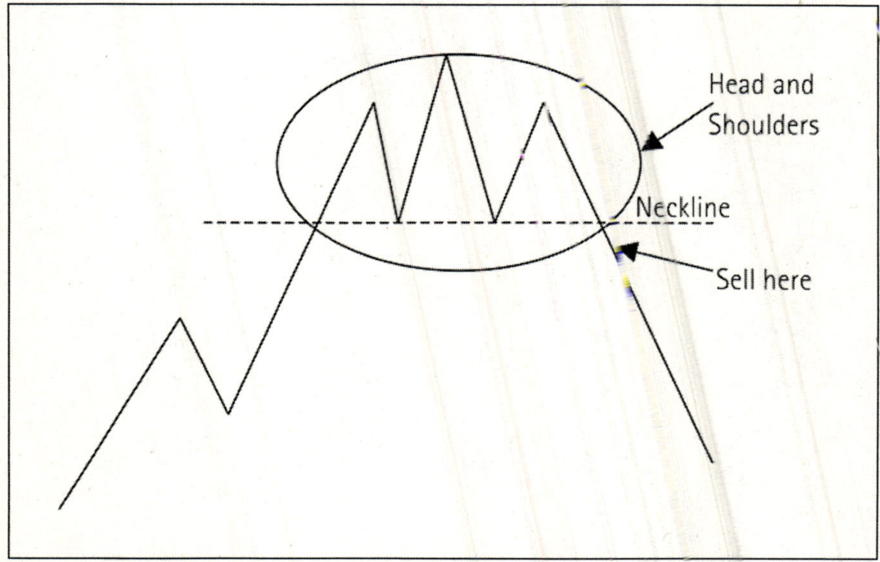

Figure 7.26: **Head and shoulders formation**

It is also important to remember that the head and shoulder patterns can be irregular. That is, the neckline can be upward sloping or downward sloping. The core idea is to exit the stock when this neckline is broken at the lowest point if you own the stock and believe that it is overvalued either intrinsically or extrinsically (*see also* Figure 7.27).

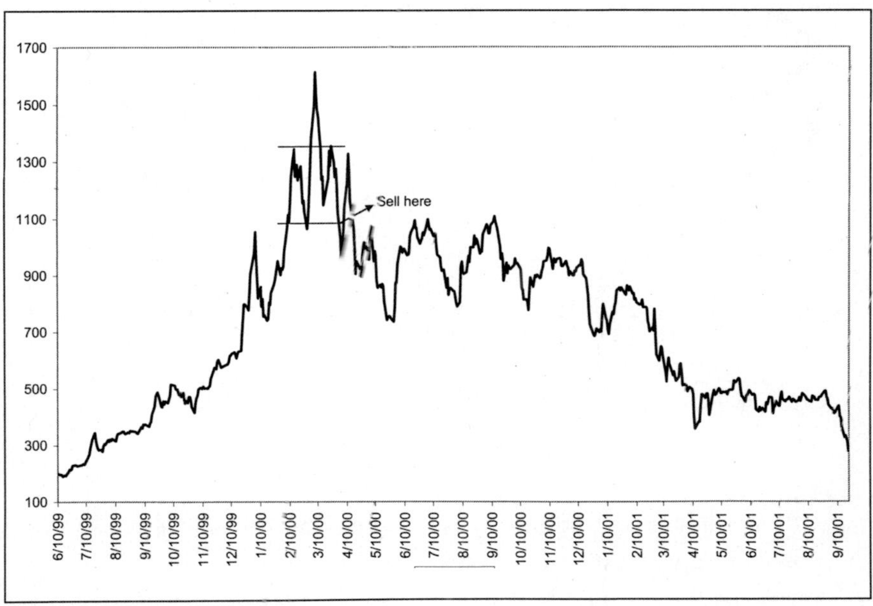

Figure 7.27: **A head and shoulders pattern in the price chart of Infosys**

Now that we have explored various patterns, I hope that it gives you an idea of how you can use charts to enhance your entries and exits rather than doing so solely on the basis of fundamentals. Technical analysis is a much vaster field than what I have covered here. I am only including information and some trading strategies that may be relevant for a long term investor who is looking to generate a multibagger return. Also remember that to generate multibaggers, you cannot rely only on technical analysis. Technical analysis rarely gives you the conviction necessary to hold something for the long term. Your conviction needs to be based in the real world. Technical analysis is only a tool that fine-tunes your timing capabilities. There are several good books in the market that offer a more in-depth look at technical analysis and if you find that this chapter intrigues you, you may want to study technicals further by reading books focused on that subject.

8

Gambling, Investment, Multi-baggers, Speculation and You

> **"The safest way to double your money is to fold it over once and put it in your pocket."** — Kin Hubbard

There is a persistently-held view that investing in the stock market is akin to gambling. A lot of very informed people mistakenly believe this to be true. Since they do not believe that there is any logic to price movements in the equity market, they believe that investing is gambling. However, let us look more closely at all three risk taking activities: gambling, speculation and investment. How are they similar to each other and how are they different?

Let us look at the similarities first:

- **Probability of Loss:** All three activities involve risk taking. That is, there is some probability that you will lose part or all of your principal in gambling, speculation and investment.

- **Potential for Rewards:** Gambling, speculation and investment are all entered into because you anticipate that you will win rather than lose.

Putting these similarities together leads to the conclusion that gambling, speculation and investment are all forays into uncertain territory. The similarity ends there. The differences, however, are monumental.

One big difference between gambling on the one hand and speculation and investing on the other is that gambling involves a very low chance of success with a high probability that your opponent will win. This is why people who build casinos can make lots of money. For example, in roulette, no matter how you bet, the probability of loss is higher than the probability of gain. Therefore, if you make enough bets, even though you may win some, net of everything, you will probably go home with less money than you came in with.

The other unique feature about gambling is that most players do not know what the odds of success are on any single bet, designed to benefit the house. By this definition, games like poker, blackjack and, to some extent, horse racing, do not fit the definition of gambling because the odds in these games can become favourable to players. In addition, skilled players will bet when the odds are in their favour — or, in the case of poker, try to bluff their opponents into believing that the odds are in their favour — and make money on average rather than lose money. However, most people enter gambles without knowing that the odds are stacked against them or, for that matter, even what the odds are. To summarize, in a gamble, most players are unaware that the odds are against them and are mathematically designed to benefit the house.

The fundamental difference between a gamble and a speculative or investment venture is that the odds are not as precise as they are in gambles. Speculation or investment is based on uncertainty, yes, because the odds are continuously shifting and cannot be precisely defined. A wide range of outcomes are indeed possible and skilled speculators and investors will change their behaviour as they are able to understand which outcomes become more likely.

At this point it becomes important to distinguish between speculating and investing. In common parlance, speculators have become evil manipulators and investors are those who are wise and somehow are better people to hang around with. However, I like two definitions of speculation:

1. "An investment operation is one which upon thorough analysis promises safety of principal and an adequate return. Operations not meeting these requirements are speculative."*

2. **Speculation:** The activity of forecasting the psychology of the market. **Speculative motive:** The object of securing profit from knowing better than the market what the future will bring forth.**

The difference between speculation and investment, as defined by Benjamin Graham, is one that promises safety of principal and an adequate return. While Graham thought that this was possible, I disagree. In any investment venture, analysis only increases the understanding of odds of success as they stand at that

---

* *Security Analysis* (1934 edition), Benjamin Graham and David Dodd

** *The General Theory of Employment, Interest, and Money*, John Maynard Keynes

point of time but does not promise any safety. If we acknowledge that analysis increases odds and if we refer to Keynes' definition of speculation, we can distinguish between investing and speculation by saying that investments perhaps depend less on what the psychology of the market is whereas speculation depends a lot on market psychology. Therefore, speculation requires that you put in the work to understand the psychology of the market whereas investment is more "fundamentals" oriented. But the big binding factor between both these, in my opinion, is that you can increase your probability of success by doing analysis either on the company itself or on the market's psychology. The fact that we can increase the probability of success ultimately distinguishes speculation and investment from gambling. In most gambles, the odds are fixed mathematically to favour the house. In speculation and investment, the astute participant can increase his or her own chances of success.

So, if gambling is at one end of the spectrum and stuffing money in a mattress is at the other end of the spectrum of risk taking, where does multibagger investing fall? Figure 8.1 (overleaf) gives you a way to analyze various risk-taking ventures. The vertical axis lays out the volatility of returns from low to high. The horizontal axis shows the ability of the participants to influence the chances of success by understanding the odds they face.

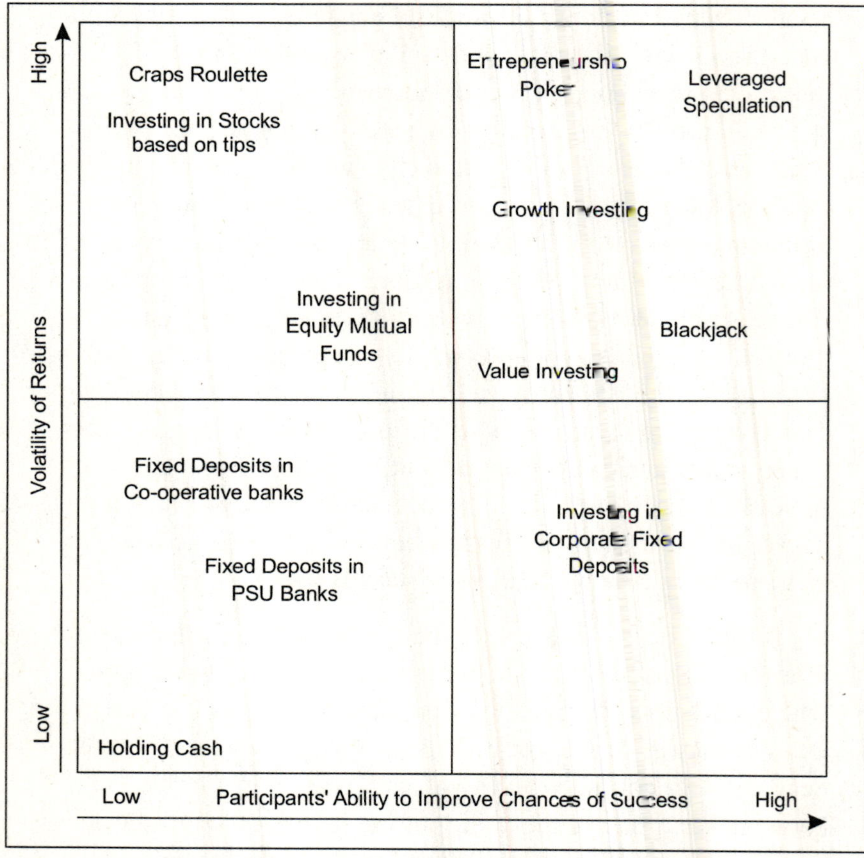

Figure 8.1: **A framework for analysis of risk-taking ventures**

The top right quadrant is the quadrant which requires continuous work and dedication and can be developed as a skill over a period of time. That is where multibagger investing lies, along with growth investing, value investing and poker. One may ask why I am putting poker in the same category as a more "serious" pursuit such as investing. That is because there are highly talented poker players who have developed the necessary knowledge and skills required to consistently win at poker, just as there are highly skilled speculators and investors. The top left quadrant is the worst place to be. Here, the volatility of returns is very high but the participant can do nothing to improve the odds. Roulette is a great example. You may win once in a while at a roulette table but the odds are stacked against you by the very design of the game. All the bets you can place in roulette have a negative expected value. This means that you will lose if you play roulette enough times. The immutable laws of probability are working against you in such games. The bottom left quadrant is a safe place to be. As an investor, you will not suffer greatly if you place your money there. The only risk is that inflation and taxes will eat away your purchasing power but you will never have much volatility of return and neither can you greatly influence the chances of success. The bottom right quadrant is totally irrelevant because if there is no volatility of return, there is no great advantage you get by increasing chances of success.

The key to success when you invest is to understand your own personality.

- Can you put in the effort to increase your own chances?
- Can you handle the volatility of returns?
- The answer to these two questions will determine whether you will be successful in doing whatever type of investment you undertake.
- If you cannot handle volatility and cannot put in the time to increase your odds of success, you should stick to bank deposits or holding cash.
- If you are able to handle volatility but do not have any time to put in any effort to improving your odds, you should put your money in an equity mutual fund.

- If you want to lose all your money but enjoy the thrill of a big win every now and then, you should take tips from all and sundry and gamble in the futures market.

How do multibaggers fit into this framework differentiating gambling, speculation and investment? Multibaggers offer you the chance to make a spectacular amount of money with a reasonable chance of success if you are willing to put in the work to identify the right companies, develop the psychology required to handle the issues surrounding the holding of a potential multibagger through its long journey and the discipline to exit at the right time. In a sense, multibaggers are like long shot roulette bets offering the highest payoff but, unlike the roulette bet, with enough information to dramatically increase your chances of success. No amount of analysis will help you in roulette in the long run. Not so in multibaggers. But in order to succeed, you need to do the hard work involved, and develop your psychology and discipline in a certain direction.

Multibaggers and Your Personality

Investing, like life, offers several paths to success. Not everyone can succeed using only one methodology. Successful examples abound of value investors, momentum investors, traders with very short term horizons, highly leveraged hedge funds, as well as very long term growth investors. Not everyone can succeed at multiple investment disciplines. A value investor may not necessarily turn into a successful leveraged speculator, just like a successful scientist will find it difficult to win an Olympic gold medal in sprinting. Various factors determine your investment success, including your risk appetite, your psychological ability to tolerate volatility, your existing financial commitments, and your ultimate financial goals. All these factors combine to create your own unique investment personality. Once you discover your investment personality, the greatest success can be achieved by staying within your investment comfort zone rather than going out of it. That is why you will notice that Warren Buffett essentially stays within his comfort zone of long term investing, George Soros stays within his comfort zone of medium term leveraged speculation, and Rakesh Jhunjhunwala, who seems to be good at both trading and long term investing, does both. Just as these investors have their personalities, the multibagger investor has a specific personality

Here are some of the characteristics of a multibagger investor:

- **Long Term Horizon:** If you check the prices of your stocks every day, you are probably not very well suited to multibagger investing. You need to think in terms of at least 5 to 10 years as your investment horizon. This means that you should not look to your multibagger investment for day-to-day excitement or entertainment. Multibaggers are not made in a day.
- **The Ability to Convert Observations from Day-to-Day Life into Investing Theses:** This means that you need to have some familiarity with the stock market. Once you observe what you think is a powerful real-world trend, you need to understand which stocks may benefit from it. For example, if you find that there is buoyancy in real estate prices, you need to quickly be able to figure out which real estate stocks may be worth buying. Or, if you see that there is a mass migration from scooters to motorcycles, you need to know which stock is likely to benefit from that trend.
- **Financial Freedom:** You have to be able to leave your potential multibagger investments alone for long periods of time. If your daughter is getting married next year, you cannot plunge into a stock hoping that it will return five times your money in one year. More likely than not, you will lose a lot of money by such

a move. Never invest money you need into a potential multibagger. And once you invest money in a potential multibagger, unless you develop reasons to believe that this stock would not in fact become a multibagger, be willing to leave it alone.

- **High Risk Appetite:** Equity markets world-wide are volatile. In India, they are like the scariest roller coaster ride invented in the world. A lot of experienced investors from the developed world cannot handle the volatility of the Indian stock market. Potential multibaggers in India tend to be more volatile than either the Sensex or Nifty. Unless you are prepared for a wild ride, and are willing to suffer stomach churning volatility, you should not try to invest in potential multibaggers.
- **Intellectual Flexibility:** Multibaggers come in different sizes, shapes — and from different industries at different time. A dogmatic investor who says that he will buy only stocks from a certain sector with a certain valuation will not be able to find, or harvest, multibaggers. If you do not like commodities, you wouldn't have been able to catch Sterlite. If you are unwilling to buy highly leveraged companies, you would not have caught Aban Offshore.

Risk Appetite

Different people have different attitude towards risk. This risk appetite can be part of their own inherent mental make up or may be forced on them due to circumstances.

Some people are inherent risk takers. They do not feel satisfied unless they are risking something constantly. A very extreme and addictive form of such risk taking can be seen in gamblers.

A lot of entrepreneurs are prudent risk takers, that is, they are willing to take a risk after a careful assessment of the odds they are facing. This risk appetite may come from either being relatively financially independent, having a great degree of confidence in oneself, or coming from a risk taking culture (such as in business families).

The risk-averse are the mirror image of these risk takers. Such risk-averse people generally do not want to hold equities, much less multibaggers. They prefer to be employed by highly stable employers. Sometimes, even risk takers are forced by circumstances to become risk averse. If a risk-taking individual has taken a huge home loan, he may be less inclined to participate in equity markets, given their very volatile nature. So his circumstances make him less risk averse.

Those who are risk averse should maintain very little exposure in their portfolio to multibaggers. Otherwise, they will lose money even on stocks which go on to become multibaggers. Risk takers may want to increase their exposure to multibaggers.

Exposure to potential multibaggers may also depend on one's present situation in life and continuing financial needs. Those with absolutely no further need for money may want to put greater than 60% of their money in potential multibaggers. But not everyone is so fortunate. Some of us continue to need money for various aspects of living. If we plunge all we have in potential multibaggers, the risk is that we may not have access to our money when we most need it either because of low liquidity or because of volatility in these multibagger stocks.

There is, typically, a direct relationship between age and risk appetite. For most people who have not made a fortune in some pursuit, the older we get, the lower our risk appetite becomes. This is because most people have increased financial commitments at an older age, such as the education of children or the need to pay for weddings or taking care of elderly parents or our own healthcare needs. So in most typical cases, it is best to maintain low exposure (10-20% of equity allocation) to multibaggers if one is over 50 years of age.

If you are below 35, your capability to handle risk is very high because you still have several years of working life ahead of you and your immediate financial commitments may not be very high. This is an ideal profile for a higher exposure to potential multibaggers (40-60% of total portfolio).

There are, however, exceptions. If you are either a professional investor or have more money than you need for your financial commitments, your exposure to multibaggers can be higher (*see* Figure 8.2).

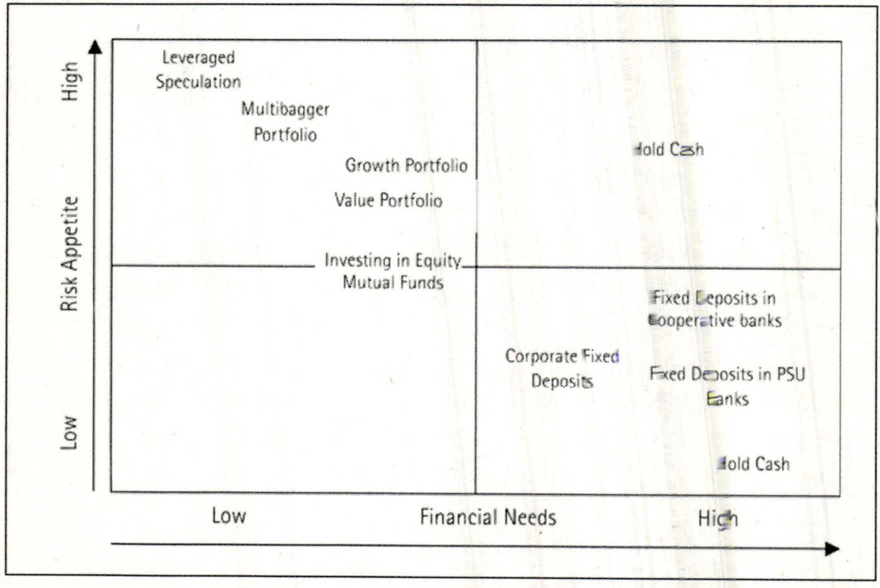

Figure 8.2: **A framework for assessing your risk-taking ability**

Psychology

The fact that you are reading this book suggests that you have a desire to make much more money than what you've already been making in stocks. However, if you do not have the right psychological make-up, it is nearly impossible to achieve a multibagger return even though you buy a stock that becomes a multibagger.

One of the key psychological traits required to achieve multibagger returns is one of total calm in the midst of mayhem in the markets. Unless you are a professional trader who knows how to get in at each intermediate bottom and get out at each intermediate top, you will find it very difficult to time a multibagger return. Stocks which go on to become multibaggers can drop like stones after you buy them before they just as abruptly recover all their losses and make huge gains. If the prospect of temporarily "losing" 70% of your money bothers you, it is best to maintain a very low exposure to multibaggers. Indian equity markets are prone to stomach churning volatility. Multibaggers, which are essentially long shots, are even more volatile than equity indices. Be prepared to be rattled in this high volatility adventure, otherwise you are nearly guaranteed to sell your potential multibaggers at the wrong time.

Accepting uncertainty is also a key psychological element of earning multibagger returns. The stock market does not work on scientific principles. It is a highly subjective field in which unpredictability and the probability of being wrong is very high. Companies that you think are duds may go on to become multibaggers and those that you think are potential multibaggers will go bankrupt. So, while one should not be rattled excessively when the entire market moves down, it is important to track the financial performance of companies that you have invested in. If they are consistently not performing well, it is best to get out.

However, this means that you will be wrong sometimes. Companies that have given several quarters of poor performance may suddenly turn around and become multibaggers. One has to be willing to tolerate this high degree of uncertainty in order to maintain one's sense of balance. If you are the type who wants predictability and certainty, you should probably maintain very low exposure to multibaggers (less than 10% of your equity allocation). However, if you are the type who can manage uncertainty, then you may want to have a moderate to high degree of exposure (30-60% of your equity exposure) to potential multibaggers.

The quest for generating multibagger returns is one prone to several pitfalls. One thing you can say for certain is that you will commit several mistakes in the process of trying to buy potential multibaggers. In a sense, it is like venture capital investing. 20% of your portfolio will generate 80% of your return. Moreover, unless you have a run of exceptional bad luck, the return generated will be higher than from the more sedate types of investing. However, an inherent psychological requirement for being successful here is to take your losses in your stride. If you are going to fret and stay away from equities for years after taking a loss, you will not be able to generate multibagger returns. However, you need to be careful and understand from your mistakes and try not to repeat them. If you blindly enter another investment without regard for its pros and cons, you are more likely a compulsive gambler than a thoughtful investor. It is important to not let your mistakes completely demoralize you but at the same time, you shouldn't turn into a reckless gambler.

Why Buy One When You Can Buy a Dozen?

In investing circles, there is a constant debate between two camps: the diversifiers and the concentrators.

The diversifiers argue that you have to have diversification in your portfolio from among many stocks and sectors so that you are not unnecessarily exposed to the risk of holding a stock with a specific event or sectoral bad news. However, diversification does not protect you from a market meltdown, like the one we had between 2008 and 2009. Also, by diversifying, an excellent return on one investment will not amount to much in the portfolio.

The concentration camp (pun not intended) argues that to get real results out of a portfolio, you need concentration, that is you need to invest very heavily in just a few stocks and sectors so that you can capture the maximum returns possible. The downside to this argument is that one disastrous investment can dramatically affect the return on your portfolio.

My team and I have often asked ourselves how this trade-off between diversification and concentration applies to multibaggers. Given the inherent volatility and unpredictability of multibaggers, we have come to the conclusion that if you want to build a multibagger portfolio, it has to be diversified. There are two primary reasons for this:

- **Unpredictability:** We have often seen that stocks that look like multibaggers go nowhere for years while those that look terrible suddenly shoot up and generate tremendous returns. This happens because of specific events that the common public will never gain knowledge of. We may believe that a certain sector is promising but the government may suddenly intervene in that sector and suck all the promise out of it. There are many possible risks to any single company, especially the smaller companies that have the profile of a potential multibagger. In order to reduce the risk of being adversely affected by any one development, it is best to think in terms of a multibagger portfolio rather than just in terms of just very few stocks.

- **Liquidity Holes:** In India, smaller stocks have very low liquidity. They don't offer the ability to get in or out very easily. This situation is compounded by the fact that a lot of small capitalization stocks have circuit filters. That is, if a price move greater than a certain percentage occurs, trades of only the opposite direction are allowed by the exchanges. This means that, say, a stock falls to its circuit filter level of 5% from the previous close, only buy orders are permitted and the sell orders are executed at the 5% circuit filter level in a queue. So, if you want to get out of the stock, you may not find any buyers. In such a situation, if one is heavily exposed to a stock and it drops to the lower circuit filter, it may not be possible to get out because the exchange will not let either you or anyone else get out. In 2008 and 2009, a lot of small capitalization stocks were frozen in the lower circuit every single day for months on end. This type of a liquidity hole can be avoided through diversification even though it means that your potential returns are somewhat diluted.

Given these two reasons, we believe that it is best to allocate capital to a group of potential multibaggers rather than to just one or two. So, whenever we talk of exposure to multibaggers, we typically think in terms of exposure to a portfolio of potential multibaggers rather than to just one stock with great characteristics. The trade-off, however, is that your multibagger portfolio as a whole may not generate as much return as a single multibagger in your portfolio.

But what is the ideal number of stocks in a multibagger portfolio? Without getting too scientific, we will suggest between 5 and 10 stocks, equally weighted. If one of the stocks starts performing aggressively, you may want to sell another stock in the portfolio to buy more of the out performer. This will increase your risk but will also increase your return. However, you may not want to do this more than once or twice otherwise the benefits of diversification will all go away.

Role of a Multibagger Portfolio in Your Portfolio

Having described the ideal multibagger investor, I would like to backtrack slightly. The characteristics described earlier in this chapter are necessary for finding and holding multibaggers. Not everyone may possess them to a great degree but all of us have these characteristics in some measure. So, even if you are an investor with very low risk appetite and are unwilling to hold for the long term, you may want to allocate a very small part of your portfolio to potential multibaggers. You can dramatically improve your investment performance by even allocating as little as 10% of your portfolio to potential multibaggers. However, there is a caveat: I am assuming that multibaggers will generate very high return. However, that may not be the case. Potential multibaggers may eat up some of your capital.

By putting a small portion of our money in multibagger type situations, you run the risk of losing all that you have put in. But if things go right, you may make significantly more money. So, the greater your risk appetite, the higher should be your allocation to multibaggers. But never forget that some of these situations may go to zero.

There is one final advantage to holding a portfolio of potential multibaggers for the long term. Under the current tax laws, long term capital gains are taxed at 0%. This means that all gains from multibaggers are tax free!

PART 2

Some Indian Multibagger Examples

In this part of the book I have included a number of examples of Indian stocks that have become multibaggers in the recent past. These detailed examples demonstrate how an investor might have identified and evaluated these multibagger return opportunities and are meant to illustrate the application of the framework of multibagger investing in real life. However, please remember that these are examples from the past and it is not being suggested that these stocks or companies can generate mega returns even in the future.

Example I — BEML

Public sector companies are usually thought of as slow, lethargic and incapable of timely, proper execution on opportunities presented to them. That doesn't sound like the characteristics one should look for in a multibagger, right? Maybe not, as BEML will show us.

Had you bought BEML in 2000, you would have made 64 times your money by 2008. That is no shabby return.

Company Background

BEML (Bharat Earth Movers Ltd.) is India's leading manufacturer of earth movers, railway coaches and defence vehicles. It was owned by the government and comes under the ambit of the Ministry of Defence. Its products include bulldozers, dump trucks, hydraulic excavators, wheel loaders, bulldozers, tyre handlers, pipe layers, rope shovels, walking draglines, motor graders, scrapers, water sprinklers, aircraft towing tractors and backhoe loaders. Most of its products are used in the construction, excavation and mining industries.

Low Market Capitalization but High P/E Ratio

In the carnage of the 2000 bear market, several good companies had their stocks beaten down to unthinkable depths. One of these was Bharat Earth Movers Ltd. (BEML). The company had sales of ₹1,330 crore but a market capitalization of only ₹123 crore. When a company has such a low price in comparison to its own sales, it is a clear sign of undervaluation. But the mere presence of value does not result in multibaggers. In order to understand BEML's potential, in 2000, it was important to understand the potential offered by the infrastructure industry. Its P/E was a relatively steep 238. However, it is important to understand that in recessions, cyclical companies like BEML see significant drops in profits and, as a result, in spite of low market capitalizations, have high price-earnings ratios. There is a very important lesson to learn from BEML. It is that the market capitalization in relation to the opportunity is more important than a simple valuation ratio in cyclical or young businesses.

Let us now examine the size of the opportunity. The infrastructure industry was nascent in 2000. India had not made significant investment in any form of infrastructure, be it roads, ports, irrigation, airports or power. The NDA coalition government proposed the Golden Quadrilateral project. This project was meant to link the four major metros in the country with international quality highways measuring 5,840 kilometres. Any road project would require massive amounts of digging, excavation and clearing. BEML made equipment for these purposes. The Golden Quadrilateral would prove to be the golden opportunity for BEML. The project was estimated to cost ₹27,000 crore. If 5%

of the project cost involved equipment, this project alone could double the size of BEML. Moreover, if the market ever decided to value the company properly, even if the price to sales multiple improved from 10% to 50%, which would still be cheap, BEML could go up anywhere between 2 and 10 times its then prevailing price. In reality, from its 2000 bottom, the company ended up appreciating more than 60 times by 2008. If all the other projects that India had to execute in order to have reasonable infrastructure were included in the opportunity size, it would be much larger. The ₹123 crore market capitalization was extremely small in relation to the size of this opportunity.

Internal Changes

In addition to the external opportunity developing, the company also undertook major internal restructuring. In December 2002, there was a change in the management. Mr. V. R. S. Natarajan took over as MD from Dr. K. Aprameyan. He initiated a restructuring program to reorganize BEML's business divisions and to foray into infrastructure and construction equipment. Until then, the company's main focus areas had been defence and mining. Rather than relying on only those two sectors, it continuously increased its range by introducing new products in the areas of infrastructure and disaster control. BEML also received an order to supply coaches for Delhi Metro project from a Korean company, Rotem. This increased focus on new products increased the size of its opportunity. The management also emphasized on improving the company's profitability. Mr. Ketan Thacker of Anagram Stock broking pointed out that the CMD of BEML had set a profit target of 8 to 10 per cent of the turnover by 2006-07, compared to the prevailing net margin of under 1 per cent.* The management change brought additional dynamism to BEML that did not exist before.

Performance

From a bottom of ₹13 in 2001, BEML rallied to a high of ₹106 in July 2002. Then it promptly lost 50% of its value by October 2002 and settled at a price of ₹48. By November 2003, it nearly quintupled from its October 2002 low to reach a price of ₹247. By May 2004, it lost 60% from its near peak to settle at ₹101. From May 2004, it began a breathtaking rally to end up at ₹1,600 by March 2006. It again fell 50% to ₹770 in 2 months. Recovering again, it went up to ₹1,775 in January 2008 when it went into a corrective phase.

This stock again reminds us of how difficult it is to hold multibaggers. It is easy to lose faith when something loses 50% of its value in a very short period of time. But you can only capture mega returns if you stick with well selected stocks in volatile times (*see* Figure I.1)

At the time that BEML bottomed out in 2001, its sales had grown at a somewhat anaemic pace of 6%. Profits actually took a nosedive in this period from ₹46 crore to ₹6 crore. These numbers would have made a purchase decision extremely difficult. The key insight that one needed in order to make this purchase decision was the absurdly low market capitalization of the company both in relation to its own sales and to the size of the

---

* 'BEML Surges on Speculative Interest', *The Business Line* 18 December 2002

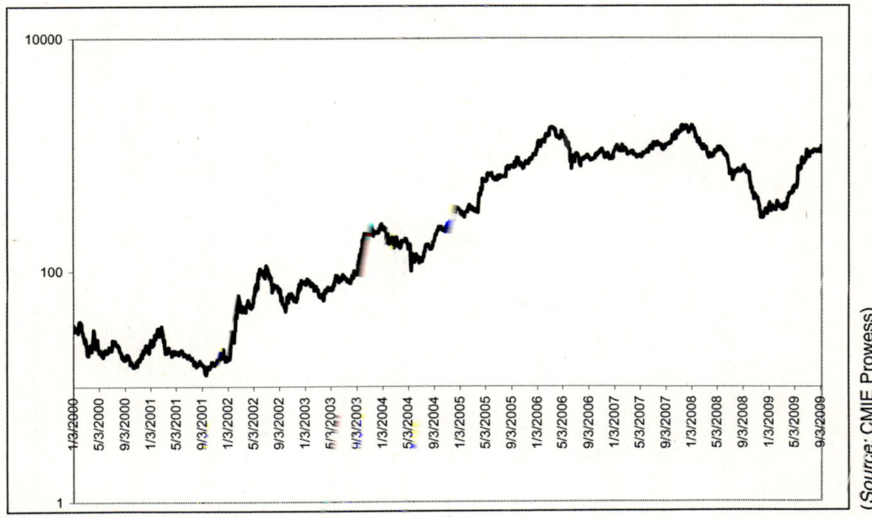

(*Source:* CMIE Prowess)

(Note: This chart is in logarithmic scale)

Figure I.1: **The price chart of BEML**

---

opportunity. The other aspect one would have to be cognizant of was the incipient infrastructure boom in the country. There were several signs that the government wanted to improve the infrastructure. An investor would have had to combine all this information and make an investment decision with a long term perspective in this stock. After the investment was made, sales continued to grow at a somewhat sedate pace of 9% per annum. In 2002, profits actually declined, making any investors nervous and precipitating a 60% decline in the stock. But profits rose at a clip of 85% per annum though there was a rough patch in 2004 when profits declined. This investment again shows the importance of not being obsessively focused on the bottom line of the company when a very large story is unfolding.

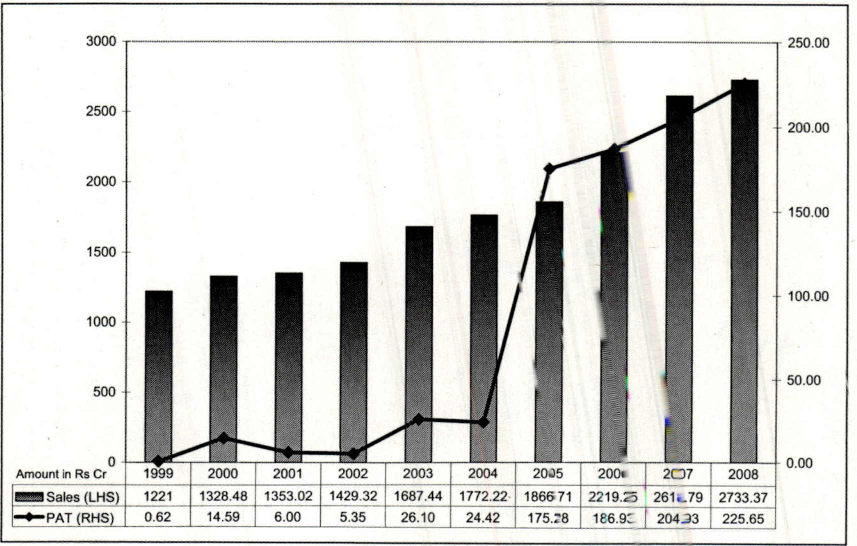

Figure I.2: **Sales and PAT of BEML**

BEML is an excellent example of how long term investment in a very large growth story pays off. There were periods of extreme turbulence in the stock and financial performance was not always excellent. But for those investors who held on patiently, keeping the long term story in mind, BEML provided excellent returns (*see* Table I.1 and Figure I.2).

Table I.1

Growth in BEML's P/E, Market Cap and Sales

	Starting (2000)	*Ending (2009)*	*CAGR*
P/E	237.78	16.64	
Market Cap (₹Cr)	123.65	4,947.16	58.59%
Sales (₹Cr)	1,221	2,726.23	10.60%

(*Source:* CMIE Prowess)

Time-line

- 1964: BEML incorporated.
- 1979: Enters into technical collaboration with Komatsu Ltd, Japan to manufacture wide range of earth moving equipment.
- 1985: Sets up dump truck division at Mysore.
- 1986: An exclusive hydraulics and power line division with R&D facility set up at Kolar Gold Field.
- 1991: Engine division set up at Mysore to manufacture heavy duty diesel engines.
- 1992: Government divests 25% stake.
- 1998: NDA government announces golden quadrilateral project as a part of NHDP.
- 2002: V. R. S. Natarajan assumes charge as CMD and announces restructuring plan.
- 2002: Announces foray into Infrastructure equipment.
- 2003: Supplies hi-tech stainless steel coaches for Delhi Metro.
- 2007: Announces foray into coal mining by forming JV with Midwest Granites Pvt. Ltd, Hyderabad and SMJ, Indonesia.
- 2007: BEML files for FPO and government's stake to come down to 54%.

Example II — Dr. Reddy's Labs

An investor in Dr. Reddy's Labs (DRL) who bought the stock for about ₹1.5 in 1990 would have made about 560 times his money by 2004. I am sure most people would agree that it was a more than adequate return! Three factors came together to produce this spectacular return:

- **Price Controls on Drugs in India:** The Government of India, in its wisdom, decided to strictly control the prices of mass-usage formulations in the 1970s. This resulted in prices in India being capped at almost 10% of international prices for the same drugs. As a result, several multinational drug companies lost interest in the Indian market, paving the way for Indian manufacturers.

- **Liberal Patent Laws in India:** The Indian Patent Act of 1970 created a process patent regime that did not recognize product patents. This meant that domestic producers could locally produce a drug that mimicked a costly drug available outside the country for a fraction of the cost as long as they followed a different process for producing it. This further reduced the attraction of India as a market for drug multinationals.

- **The Balance of Payments Crisis in 1991:** Thanks to India's poor economic policies and the first Gulf War, India could not afford to pay for its exports and was forced to devalue its currency. Over the next 10 years, the rupee plummeted from ₹18 to the dollar to ₹48. This created a very positive atmosphere for capable exporters. The drug industry was one of the prime beneficiaries since they had learned the ropes of production in the Indian market and those with execution skills rapidly converted to exports.

Established in 1984 by Dr. Anji Reddy, DRL initially focused on bulk drug exports. The company had already attracted a lot of attention by 1990. It was considered a rising star of the nascent drug industry in India. The company had developed a unique skill of scaling up production of what were then considered sunrise drugs and rapidly changing their products to suit the market's needs. In 1990, it had just begun exporting new drugs Norfloxacin and Ciprofloxacin.

Low Valuation

The market capitalization of DRL in 1990 was ₹13 crore. Even if you completely ignored the export market and only focused on the domestic market, and even if every Indian spent ₹10 on medicines per year, the market size was roughly ₹700 crore for one year's sales. At ₹13 crore market capitalization, it was not even 2% of the industry's potential sales in India alone. If you extended this same logic to the rest of the world, you would arrive at a very conservative market size of roughly ₹3,500 crore per year. In reality, just the American drug market was much larger.

It is pertinent to ask if you could have foreseen the future in 1990 and made a bet on DRL. Even in 1990, DRL had a reputation of being a great performer. Sales grew from ₹16 crore in 1988-89 to ₹53 crore in 1990-1991. Profits in the same period grew from ₹71 lakh to ₹2.63 crore. These were spectacular increases. Moreover, DRL had a reputation of being able to identify trends in the marketplace and change their product mix accordingly. They rapidly introduced new products, scaled them up as demand for them increased and phased out others as demand waned. The company's agility was demonstrated to some extent in their phenomenal sales and profit growth. Moreover, the company was valued at less than 25% of its sales even though it had grown by more than 200% in the past two years. Any which way you looked at it, it was undervalued.

Volatility

While staying invested in the company, an investor would have experienced his fair share of volatility. The price dropped from ₹2.6 to ₹2.2 in 1991. In 1992, it dropped from ₹19 to ₹13. After rising again to ₹42, it dropped all the way to ₹23 in 1993, it again rose to ₹118 in 1994 only to begin a steady descent to ₹39 in 1995. The stock then began an inexorable rise all the way to ₹421 in 2000 but dropped very quickly to ₹239 in the same year. From the 2000 low, the stock appreciated to ₹840 by 2006. This ride would not have been easy for most investors who watched their gain or loss incessantly. In fact, most people would have booked profits too early instead of staying invested for the long term.

This volatility was a result of various market disturbances as well as changes in the company's business. DRL went from being a bulk drug exporter to a formulations exporter to a generics manufacturer to a patent litigator. The company continuously evolved and its P&L account either suffered or benefited from these various developments. The company entered the big league by licensing its anti-diabetic molecule in 1997 to Novo Nordisk for an up-front payment. A similar deal was done again in 1998, again with Novo Nordisk. DRL established itself as not just a volume manufacturer but as a company capable of conducting research that would be purchased by large global pharmaceutical companies.

DRL grew in this period from sales of ₹26 crore to ₹4,403 crore. They never had a year of declining sales even though sales growth varied from year to year. Profits dipped at various points but on the whole exhibited a spectacular annual growth rate of 45% from 1991 to 2007. DRL is another example of patience paying off, and how! (*see also* Table II.1, Figures II.1 and II.2).

Table II.1

Growth in DRL's P/E, Market Cap and Sales

	Starting (1990)	*Ending (2009)*	*CAGR*
P/E	17.37	22.77	
Market Cap (₹cr)	13	13,421.16	41.70%
Sales	26.23	4,531.5	29.38%

(*Source:* CMIE Prowess)

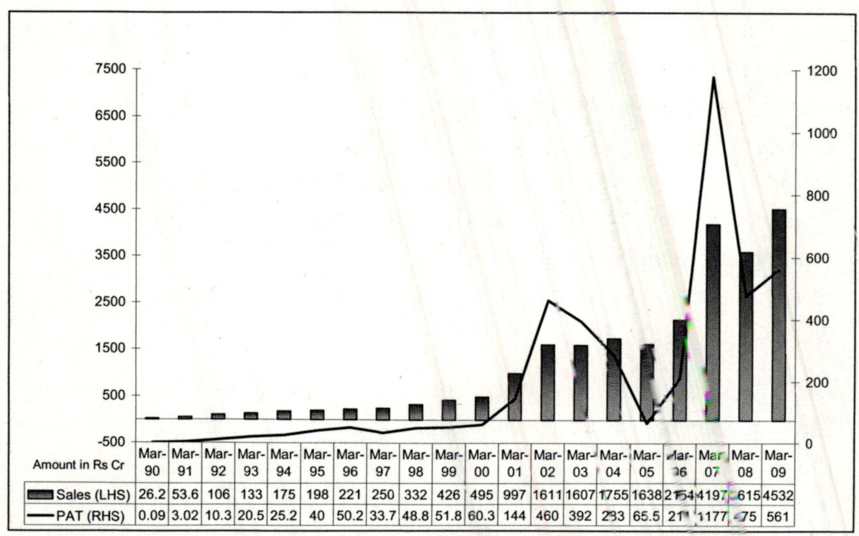

Amount in Rs Cr	Mar-90	Mar-91	Mar-92	Mar-93	Mar-94	Mar-95	Mar-96	Mar-97	Mar-98	Mar-99	Mar-00	Mar-01	Mar-02	Mar-03	Mar-04	Mar-05	Mar-06	Mar-07	Mar-08	Mar-09
Sales (LHS)	26.2	53.6	106	133	175	198	221	250	332	426	495	997	1611	1607	1755	1638	2154	4197	[illegible]615	4532
PAT (RHS)	0.09	3.02	10.3	20.5	25.2	40	50.2	33.7	48.8	51.8	60.3	144	460	392	233	65.5	21[illegible]	1177	[illegible]75	561

Figure II.1: **Sales and PAT of Dr. Reddy's Laboratories**

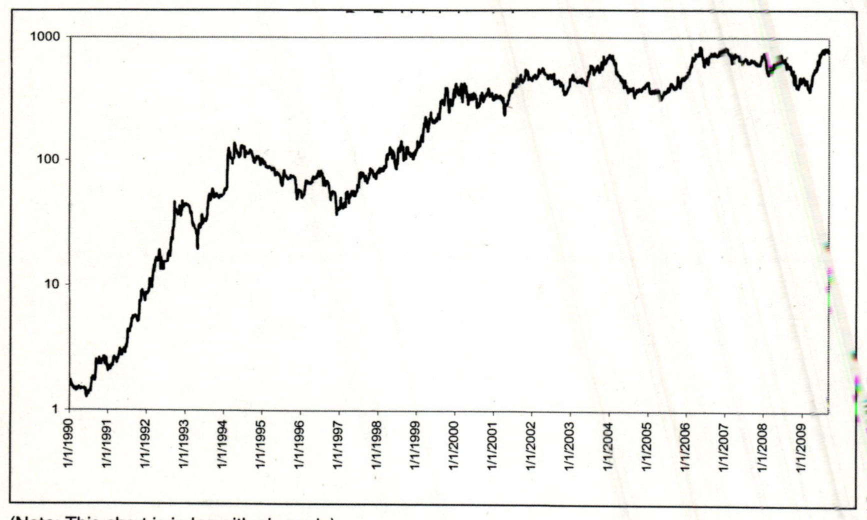

(Note: This chart is in logarithmic scale)

Figure II.2: **The price chart of Dr. Reddy's Laboratories**

Time-line

- 1988: Acquires Benzex Labs.
- 1994: Makes GDR Issue of US$48 million.
- 1995: Sets up subsidiary in Hong Kong and JV in Russia.
- 1999: Acquires Chennai-based American Remedies Ltd.
- 2000: Merger of Cheminor Drugs Ltd and American Remedies Ltd. Becomes third largest pharma company in India with a turnover of ₹1,000 crore.
- 2001: Becomes the first Asia Pacific pharmaceutical company, outside Japan, to list on New York Stock Exchange.

  Launches its first generic product, Ranitidine, in the US market.
- 2002: Acquires BMS Laboratories Limited and Meridian Healthcare, UK.
- 2003: Launches Ibuprofen, first generic product to be marketed under "Dr. Reddy's" label in the US.
- 2005: Acquires Roche's API Business with a total investment of USD 59 million.

  Announces unique partnership for commercialization of ANDAs with ICICI Venture.
- 2006: Revenues touch USD 1 billion in December 2006.

  Obtains its second 180-day marketing exclusivity for Ondenesetron Hydrochloride Tablets.
- 2007: Becomes the No. 1 pharmaceutical company in India in turnover and profitability.

Example III — Hero Honda

Back in the 1980s, anyone who couldn't afford a car would try to order a Bajaj scooter. Thanks to the license raj, which restricted capacity expansions, the waiting period for a Bajaj scooter was no less than 12 years. The other options were to buy motorcycles built by Enfield, Jawa or Rajdoot. However, except for the Enfield, these motorbikes were two-stroke fuel guzzlers and with largish engines. In 1985, Hero Honda launched its four-stroke fuel efficient 100cc motorbike. Thanks to the government's opening up of the two wheeler sector, the Hero Group was able to form a JV with Honda to bring Honda's technologically advanced fuel efficient motorbikes to India. A few months earlier, Hero Honda, had made its first public offering. Would you have bought the stock? If you did, you would have been a very happy investor.

For an investor in 1985, it would have been a difficult call to buy Hero Honda. Neither Enfield nor Jawa nor Rajdoot showed much customer acceptance. It would have been very easy to write off Hero Honda as a speculative venture. There were not enough data points to make this an easy decision. By 1993, though, it had become quite obvious that incremental growth in the two-wheeler market came from motorbikes and not scooters. Motorbikes were sleeker, more fuel-efficient, more easily available and were clearly becoming the transport option of choice for millions of Indians. Anyone who wanted mobility was starting to choose motorbikes over other vehicles. Had all those buyers of bikes bought the Hero Honda stock instead, they would have reaped a gain of 72 times their original investment by March 2008.

Company Background

Hero Cycles was the largest maker of bicycles in the world. In 1984, they established a joint venture with Honda of Japan to bring 100cc motorbikes to India. India, at the time, was a scooter dominated market. Bajaj Auto had a stranglehold on the scooter market in India. Hero Honda's first motorbike rolled off the assembly line in 1985. Unfortunately for the company, in 1986 the yen appreciated significantly against the rupee and, suddenly, the imported components of the motorbike became very expensive. In the first couple of years, Hero Honda lost money on every motorbike they sold. However, by 1991, the yen depreciated and Hero Honda started making money. By 1990, they became the dominant maker of motorbikes in India.

However, by the 1990s, Bajaj Auto had also woken up from its stupor. It started producing motorbikes in a joint venture with Kawasaki. In 1994, Hero Honda's technology sharing agreement with Honda was renewed. However, tensions between Honda and Hero Honda stymied growth for a couple of years in the mid-1990s. In the meanwhile, Bajaj Auto also launched a four-stroke motorbike backed by an aggressive advertising campaign.

Between 1993 and 2008, Hero Honda's sales grew from ₹271 crore to ₹11,553 crore. Profits grew from ₹16 crore to ₹857 crore during the same period. The stock went from ₹9 in 1993 to ₹770 in March 2008 (*see* Figure III.1).

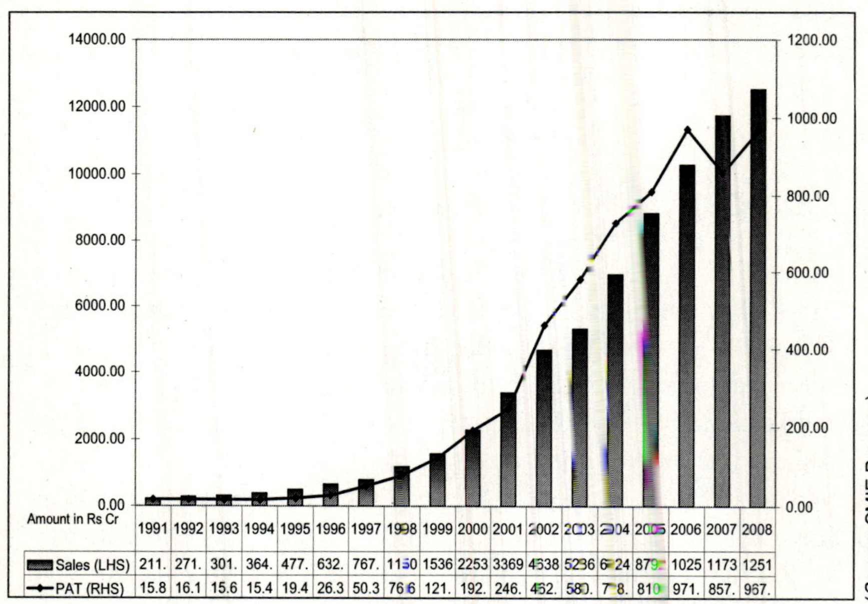

	1991	1992	1993	1994	1995	1996	1997	1998	1999	2000	2001	2002	2003	2004	2005	2006	2007	2008
Sales (LHS)	211.	271.	301.	364.	477.	632.	767.	1150	1536	2253	3369	4638	5236	6924	879[illegible]	1025	1173	1251
PAT (RHS)	15.8	16.1	15.6	15.4	19.4	26.3	50.3	76.6	121.	192.	246.	452.	580.	728.	810.	971.	857.	967.

Figure III.1: **Sales and PAT of Hero Honda Financials**

Unrecognized Change

The key issue to have recognized in Hero Honda is that there was a perceptible shift in consumer preferences from scooters to motorbikes. The price rise in fuel prices due to the first Gulf War, while scary from a stock market perspective, heightened the need for fuel efficiency. Hero Honda was the dominant producer of fuel efficient four-stroke motorbikes and for someone who wanted to take advantage of this trend, it was one of the two options. An investment in 1993 in TVS Motors would have returned 30 times the original amount.

Low Valuation Compared to Market Opportunity

A billion Indians needed some form of transportation and, yet, Hero Honda's market capitalization was only ₹200 crore. At the time, motorbikes cost around ₹20,000. Even if 1% of the total male population opted to purchase motorbikes, the market size for motorbikes was around 10 million units. This implied a potential market size of ₹20,000 crore. But Hero Honda was valued at only 1% of that. At the time, Hero Honda had sales of ₹270 crore and traded at a P/E of 20.

The Purchase Decision

Buying at the nadir of the market has tremendous advantages in delivering returns. But market bottoms become obvious only in hindsight. However, the news for Hero Honda could not have been worse in 1993. The issue was further complicated by the fact that the Harshad Mehta scam had just come out and the Sensex had suffered an astounding crash from a high of ₹4,467 in 1992 to ₹2,036 in 1993. The decision making would have been further complicated by the fact that between 1990 and 1992, the automobile industry suffered a massive recession because of the sudden jump in oil prices due to the first Gulf War and also the macroeconomic problems in India. Hero Honda had just shown a decline in volumes in 1992. In this context, even the bravest investor would be skittish about buying Hero Honda. However, purchase decisions at times like these are the most rewarding ones.

The Holding Period

Even if one had been brave enough to purchase Hero Honda in 1993, there were several points during which it was easy to lose faith in the stock. When growth stagnated in 1995, it would have been natural to want to switch. At one point in 1995, the stock fell from a peak of ₹46 to ₹19, a fall of 60%, which could have terrified most investors. It fell again from a peak of ₹301 in July 1999 to a low of ₹124 in April 2001, another fall of 60%. Between March 2002 and April 2003, it fell from ₹390 to ₹200, a 48% fall. Like all multibaggers, this tested investors' conviction several times but only rewarded the most faithful of investors with its 72-fold return (*see* Figure III.2 and Table III.1).

Table III.1

Growth in Hero Honda's P/E, Market Cap and Sales

	Starting (1991)	*Ending (2009)*	*CAGR*
P/E	10.43	22.03	
Market Cap	111.82	33,318.85	42.77%
Sales	211.88	12,518.83	29.04%

(*Source*: CMIE Prowess)

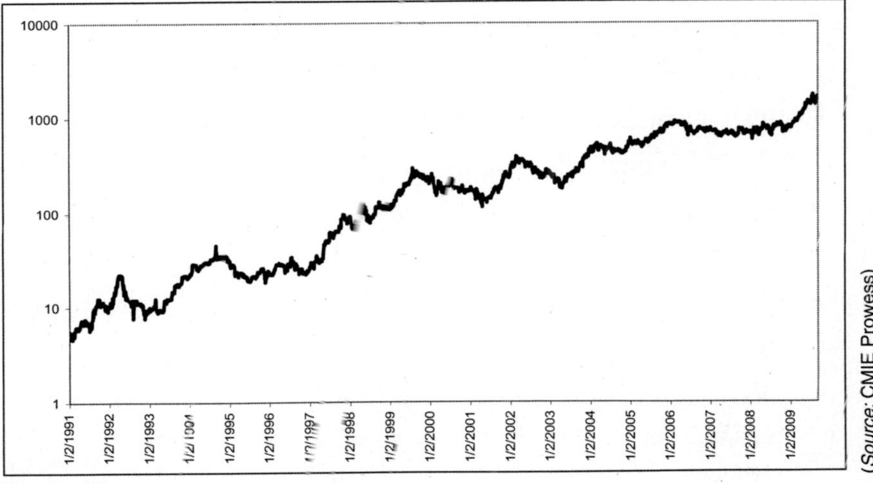

(Note: This chart is in logarithmic scale)

(*Source:* CMIE Prowess)

Figure III.2: **The price chart of Hero Honda Motors Ltd**

Time-line

- 1984: Hero Honda Motors was incorporated as a JV between Hero Cycles Pvt. Ltd. and Honda Motors, Japan.
- 1985: India's first four-stroke 100cc bike rolls out of the Hero Honda assembly line.
- 1986: Expands capacity from 1,20,000 vehicles per annum to 1,50,000 vehicles per annum.
- 1989: Introduces new model, Sleek.
- 1990: Introduces new model CD 100 SS for semi rural markets and achieves market share of 46%.
- 1994: Doubles capacity to 2,40,000 vehicles per annum and sets a new plant with a capacity of 1,50,000 vehicles per annum at Gurgaon.

- 1995: Technical collaboration with Honda Motors renewed and extended till 2004.
- 1997: Launches Honda Street suitable for congested urban traffic conditions.
- 1998: Sets up plant in Brazil to manufacture Hero Winner Scooters.
- 1999: Launches CBZ with a new feature of Transient Power Fuel Control System.
- 2000: Forms JV with US' Briggs Stratton to manufacture transmission systems and engines for two- and three-wheelers.
- 2000: Launches upgraded version of Honda Street.
- 2001: Launches Passion.
- 2002: Becomes world's largest two wheeler manufacturer by selling 1.3 mn vehicles in 2001. Launches Ambition, a 133 cc bike and Smart a 75 cc step through bike.
- 2003: Launches CD Dawn, its cheapest bike, Karisma 233 CC 16.8 bhp and launches co-branded credit card with SBI cards.
- 2004: Renews alliance with Honda Motors.
- 2005: Launches its first scooter, Pleasure, and the 150-cc Achiever.
- 2006: Launches CBZ variant X-treme, Glamour and Passion Plus limited edition.

Example IV — Infosys

Indian investors have a lot to thank Saddam Hussein and the first Gulf War for. Thanks to Hussein's ill-advised invasion of Kuwait and the subsequent war led by the United States, remittances from Indian workers in the Persian Gulf dropped precipitously. Simultaneously, crude oil prices shot up dramatically, making it difficult for India to pay for its oil imports. Both these factors put together created a balance of payments crisis in the country. In plain English, India could not pay for its foreign purchases with the money it earned from its exports. As a result, in 1991 India had to pledge its gold for foreign exchange. The Indian rupee was devalued and the government made conscious efforts to encourage exports in order to earn foreign exchange. Things never looked so bleak.

Out of this bleakness emerged one of India's great entrepreneurial successes: Infosys Technologies. N. R. Narayana Murthy and six other entrepreneurs came together to found Infosys Technologies in 1981 with ₹10,000 borrowed from Murthy's wife. The core activity of the company was to write software code for clients. Upon getting its first client, Data Basics Corp. in 1983, Infosys moved to Bangalore. The company bought its first minicomputer, a Data General 32-bit MV3000 to serve this client. Though Infosys was gaining some traction, its early days were not smooth. Infosys found a marketing partner in Kurt Salomon Associates in the late 1980s but this partnership unravelled by 1989, creating a crisis for the company. One of the founders, Ashok Arora, quit in frustration at this point. The other founders stayed on and struggled.

In 1993, Infosys decided to go public at a price of ₹96 (unadjusted for splits / bonuses / rights). The issue was barely subscribed but finally scraped through, getting oversubscribed by 1.06 times. At the time, most people in financial markets thought that Infosys was a fly-by-night operator. How wrong they were! Those who bought Infosys in 1993 would have earned a return of 245 times their original investment.

Unrecognized Change

A confluence of events, combined with Infosys' superior execution capability, changed the face of Indian IT forever. First, India was desperate to export in order to generate foreign exchange. In an effort to facilitate this, the Indian government devalued the rupee. In fact, the rupee started a multi-year downward slide against the dollar. From a high of ₹18 in 1991, the rupee slid to ₹48 by 2000. This was great for those who exported. It was especially great for Infosys because it coincided with a dramatic time in the global IT industry, which was rapidly growing at the time.

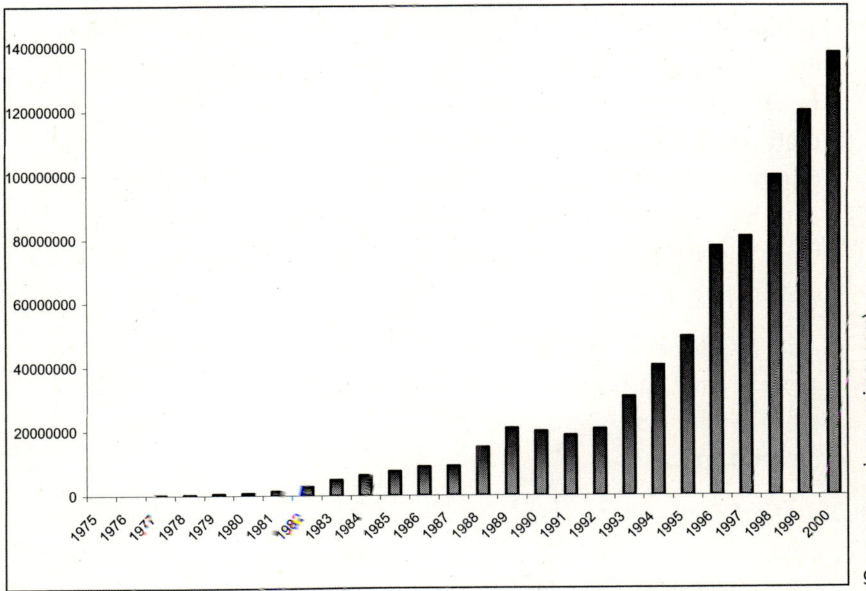

(Source: www.jeremyreimer.com)

Figure IV.1: **Chart showing global computer penetration**

Second, as the chart in Figure IV.1 shows, computers were making their presence felt in every enterprise and every individual's life globally. By 1992, computers had become an indispensable part of both personal and work life in the developing world. Enterprises had adopted reasonably complex systems that worked on varied platforms. The personal computer had also brought computing to the masses and increased the type of applications that computers were used for. PCs had become extremely cheap and very powerful and started spreading like wildfire. Computers were starting to become prevalent in most work environments, including in India. Moreover, companies like Microsoft had gone public a few years earlier, making Bill Gates an instant billionaire. So, the alert observer would have noticed that computers were a large opportunity. People started buying home computers so that they could do taxes, play computer games, write letters, etc. The graphical user interface that matured with Windows 3.0 in 1991 made the PC a reasonably easy to use device and dramatically increased penetration. The widespread use of computers for everything from accounting to word processing to entertainment was a change that went unrecognized in 1992 in India. Those who perceived this change could have benefited enormously from it.

As volumes rose and the rupee fell, Infosys's sales and profits grew dramatically. Sales grew from ₹9.38 crore in 1992 to ₹884 crore while profits grew from ₹2.25 crore to ₹293 crore during the same period.

A third factor that helped was that the government of India announced an income tax holiday for software exporters until the year 2009. All these factors came together to create explosive growth in Infosys.

Low Valuations

Both the intrinsic and extrinsic valuation of Infosys was very low at the time that it went public in 1993. It traded at a Price / Earnings ratio of 15.28, and a market capitalization of ₹53.63 crore. For a company that had grown its sales and profits by over 50% the previous year, the Price / Earnings ratio was very undemanding. Arriving at the external opportunity is slightly more difficult. A simple way to arrive at the total market for computers in the USA was to make some crude assumptions. If we assumed that computers would penetrate half the homes in the USA, the number of units sold would have been around 150 million. If the cost of software on each computer was $100, this was a $15 billion opportunity. The exchange rate at the time was ₹30, so this could have been a ₹4,500 crore opportunity. However, Infosys served the corporate market, not the home user market. A very large enterprise player like EDS had a market capitalization of $16 billion at the time. A much smaller player like Keane had a market capitalization of $[illegible]27 million. So Infosys' market capitalization was not very demanding at all. However, it is not possible to arrive at a strict numbers valuation in a dynamic market like technology. One would have had to use gut to understand that ₹53 crore was very low compared to the size of the opportunity (*see* Table IV.1 and Figures IV.2 and IV.3).

Table IV.1

Growth in Infosys P/E, Market Cap and Sales

	1995	*2009*	*CAGR*
P/E	30.87	21.20	
Market Cap (₹cr)	308.37	126076	49.32%
Sales (₹cr)	55.42	20297	48%

(*Source:* CMIE Prowess)

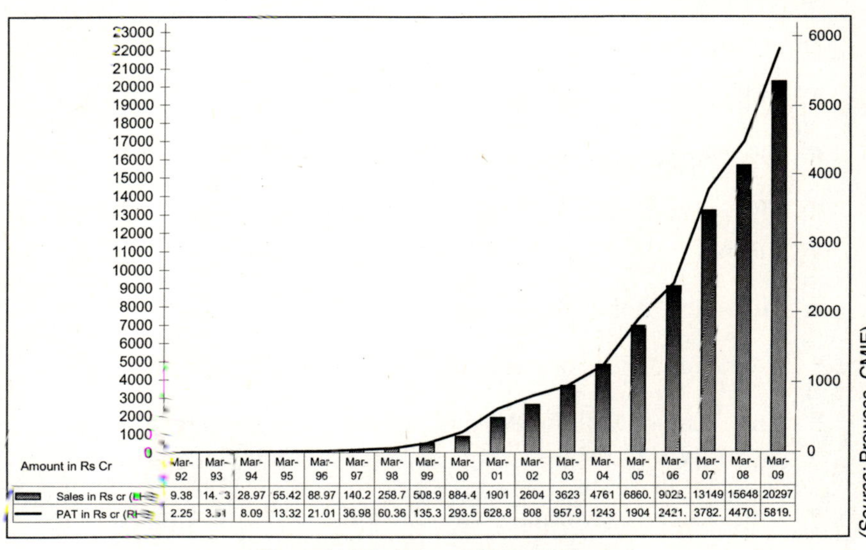

Figure IV.2: **Sales and PAT of Infosys**

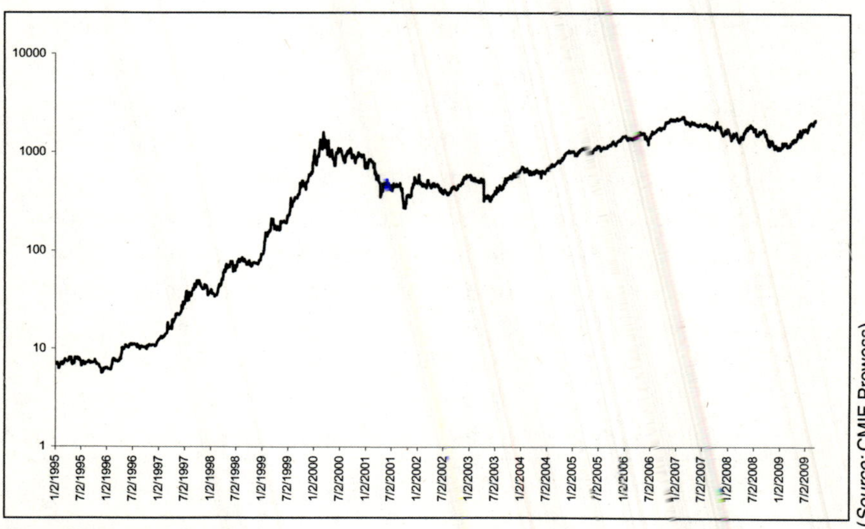

(*Source:* CMIE Prowess)

(Note: This chart is in log scale)

Figure IV.3: **The price chart of Infosys**

Time-line

- 1993: Public issue announcement.
- 1994: Announces bonus issue in the ratio of 1:1.
- 1997: Announces its plans for an ADR issue up to US$ 75 million.

  Announces bonus issue in the ratio of 1:1.
- 1999: Announces bonus issue in the ratio of 1:1.
- 2001: Enters MoU with Andhra Pradesh Government for establishing a Software Development campus at Hyderabad.
- 2002: Receives Motilal Oswal Award for Wealth Creation for 1996-2001, and Mr. Nandan Nilekani becomes the new CEO of the company.

- 2003: Announces strategic technology partnership with First Bank of Nigeria Plc. (FBN).
- 2004: Turnover touches USD 1 billion.
- 2006: Announces bonus issue in the ratio of 1:1.

Example V — Kalpataru Power Transmission Ltd.

In 2008, the power sector had a bad odour in the Indian stock market. Amidst extremely high expectations, Reliance Power's shares listed at a significant discount to the issue price. People were very sour on the industry and felt that the entire sector was overvalued. It is perhaps only fitting that we should remind them that had someone invested in the Kalpataru Power Transmission Ltd. in January 2002, by 1 January 2008, he would have made 233 times his money. It doesn't end there. Had anyone bought either Jyoti Structures or RPG Transmission, they would still have made 57 times or 107 times their money, respectively

Why did the market reward investors in these stocks so much? Simple reason; these stocks were woefully undervalued compared to the opportunity in 2002. The combined market capitalization of Kalpataru, Jyoti Structures, KEC International and RPG Transmission in 2002 was ₹69 crore. This market capitalization seems very low in a country of 1 billion people with a severe power shortage. The potential for this industry was enormous. The market was valuing the total power transmission contractor industry at less than 69 paisa per person living in India. This is a great example of how the market from time to time undervalues an entire sector.

Kalpataru was engaged in the manufacture of towers and building electrical transmission lines. Between the years 1993 and 2000, it had already demonstrated its dramatic growth. In this period, Kalpataru's revenues quadrupled from ₹40 crore to ₹165 crore. Profits increased more than seven-fold from ₹2 crore to ₹15 crore. However, sentiment in this sector was badly affected despite the domestic opportunity because of sanctions imposed on India by multilateral funding agencies after the nuclear tests conducted in 1998. This lack of funding was part of the reason for the severe undervaluation of this sector. Funding problems also meant that, by 2000, 88% of the revenues for Kalpataru were coming from exports. Kalpataru's nascent real estate business was also experiencing execution problems, which resulted in further uncertainty about the future of the company.

Most Indian state electricity boards (SEBs) looked extremely vulnerable and people considered them to be very poor credit risks. Most of them had no money to pay their suppliers. Things looked extremely bleak for the power sector as a whole. In addition to these issues, India reneged on its agreement with Enron, which subsequently went bankrupt, leaving behind a new power plant in Dabhol. Other high profile foreign investors in the generation sector, Mirant and AES decided to leave the country. Peak power shortages were very high and problems like pilferage were rampant. Moreover, transmission and distribution losses were very high, at rates of over 25%. There were also substantial subsidy schemes in almost every state, which further curtailed the efficiency of the industry.

The period between 2000 and 2002 was terrible for most stocks and Kalpataru was no exception. But there were a few company specific issues which resulted in even lower stock prices. Both sales and profits declined in 2001 because of the lack of domestically available funds for transmission projects as well as competitive pressures and pressure on raw materials. The stock bottomed at ₹8 in 2002. At this price, it was trading at a 1 P/E! Kalpataru's sales were ₹159 crore but its market capitalization was ₹18 crore. For someone who was perceptive and value-focused, this was a great opportunity.

Unrecognized Change

During this period, Kalpataru focused more on the international market. Since margins were very tight in the pure tower supply business, it made efforts to convert itself into a turnkey contractor. This resulted in a fundamental shift in its business model. The potential for margins increased since the value they added to their customers was much higher. Moreover, even as the stock was hitting new lows, the domestic scenario in India began to change for the better.

In 2000-01, the government announced the Accelerated Power Development Program (APDP). This program was targeted at renovating thermal and hydro generation stations and improving the efficiency of the transmission and distribution network. A focused investment program was undertaken in 63 districts under this scheme. The Government of India finally decided to act and entered into a Memorandum of Understanding with 19 states which undertook to reform the power sector in their states in a time-bound fashion. A one-time settlement of dues from the SEBs was also organized by the government. The Electricity Bill of 2001 was passed, which undertook a series of reforms and provided state governments with flexibility to reform the transmission and distribution sector.

In 2003, the APDP was modified to become the Accelerated Power Development and Reforms Program. The scope of this program was to improve the transmission and distribution system in the country by investing in the transmission and distribution infrastructure as well as providing an incentive for utilities to reduce losses. In addition to regular investments, the APDRP specifically focused on the use of IT to improve distribution efficiency. APDRP also outlined a funding program to ensure that money was available to implement the upgradations. As part of the incentive to improve T&D efficiency, APDRP provided 100% of funds required to pay out the incentive. Moreover, the APDRP outlined strict guidelines for dispersal of funds so that funds would not be stuck with state governments while utilities still suffered from lack of money. APDRP was a significant trigger that was set in place for improving the power sector.

The perceptive and alert investor would have understood once the APDRP was announced that there was true intent to improve the power situation in the country and that transmission and distribution infrastructure would be upgraded. This, combined with extraordinarily low valuation of companies involved in this sector, were screaming buy signals to those following action in this sector.

Volatility

As with a lot of other multibaggers, this stock experienced its fair share of volatility. It dropped 20% from its 2002 peak in 2003. After it recovered and trended higher, it dropped by 40% from its peak in 2004. It fell another 40% from its peak in 2006. But nerves of steel are required to generate dramatic returns and this company further strengthens the case for ignoring short term movements in share prices. As of the time of writing, it is not clear whether the stock is a buy. At ₹5,000 crore market capitalisation, it is neither very cheap nor very attractively priced. It has dropped significantly from its 2008 peak of ₹1,933. However, we believe that Kalpataru, unless it dramatically corrects right now, does not offer multibagger potential. At best it can offer returns that the market offers. At worst, it probably offers more debt-like returns (*see* Table V.1 and Figures V.1 and V.2).

Table V.1

Growth in Kalpataru Power Transmission Ltd. P/E, Market Cap, Sales and Institutional Holding

	Starting (2002)	*Ending (2009)*	*CAGR*
P/E	1.03	22.83	
Market Cap (₹cr)	18.74	2225.73	97.87%
Sales (₹cr)	159.03	1912.01	31.83%
Institutional Holding	7%	19.92%	

(*Source:* CMIE Prowess)

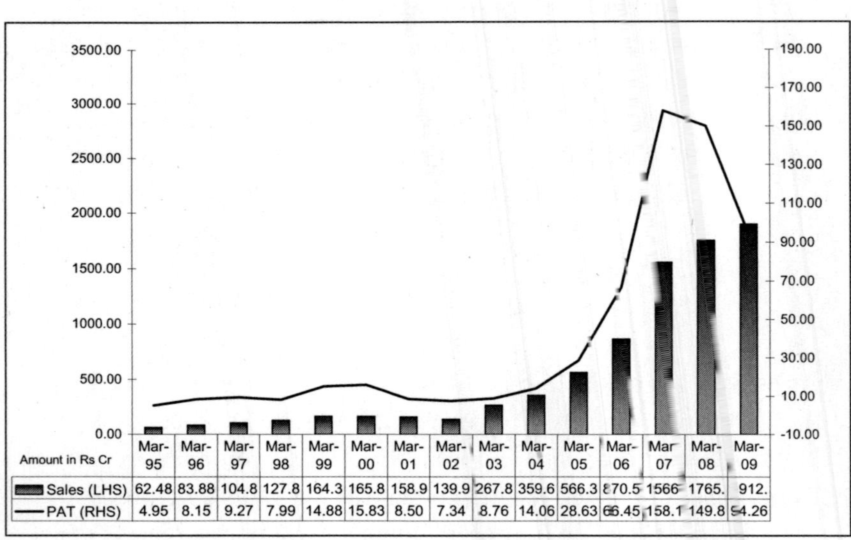

Amount in Rs Cr	Mar-95	Mar-96	Mar-97	Mar-98	Mar-99	Mar-00	Mar-01	Mar-02	Mar-03	Mar-04	Mar-05	Mar-06	Mar-07	Mar-08	Mar-09
Sales (LHS)	62.48	83.88	104.8	127.8	164.3	165.8	158.9	139.9	267.8	359.6	566.3	870.5	1566	1765.	912.
PAT (RHS)	4.95	8.15	9.27	7.99	14.88	15.83	8.50	7.34	8.76	14.06	28.63	66.45	158.1	149.8	94.26

(*Source:* Prowess, CMIE)

Figure V.1: **Sales and PAT of Kalpataru Power Transmission**

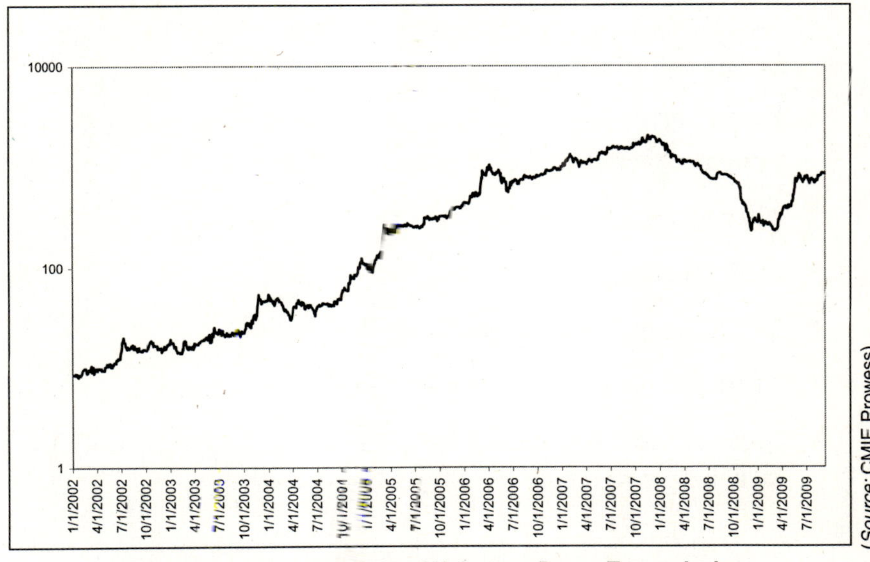

(*Source:* CMIE Prowess)

Figure V.2: **The price chart of Kalpataru Power Transmission**

Time-line

- 1981: Company incorporated as HT Power Structures Pvt. Ltd.
- 1994: Initial Public Offering over subscribed 8 times.
- 1998: Government allows private sector participation in power transmission.
- 1998: The Electricity Regulatory Commission Act, 1998.
- 1998: Mirant and AES, foreign generation companies, withdraw investments due to the inability of state electricity boards to pay their dues.
- 2001: The Electricity Bill 2001 introduced in Parliament.
- 2001: Government announces Accelerated Power Development Program (APDP).

- 2001: Kalpataru awarded project of 1,150 kms of 400kv line by Powergrid, India.
- 2003: APDP modified to become the Accelerated Power Development and Reforms Program (APDRP).
- 2005: Kalpataru diversifies into power distribution.
- 2005: Acquires equity stake in JMC Projects.
- 2005: Company enters into oil pipeline contracts.
- 2006: Company announces bonus issue in the ratio of 1: 1.
- 2006: Private placement of 47,77,000 equity shares of ₹10 each at a premium of ₹717.00 per equity share.

Example VI — Moser Baer

Even the most patient and experienced investor would have had moments of despair in holding this stock through the period of its becoming a multibagger. Moser Baer is an example of the tenacity that it may take in order to generate multibaggers. Even if you had nerves of steel to hold it through its volatility, at various points doubts about the demise of its technology-dependent business model would have made holding or even buying very difficult. However, this multibagger is a great demonstration of how faith in management can pay off for the patient investor. The secret to Moser's great performance is the capability of management to keep changing the company's business to suit changing times.

The company was started in 1983 with the intention of manufacturing time recorders and metal furniture. After several years of being in this business with limited success, Puri chanced upon the floppy disk business in the 1980s. However, those were the days of the license raj and Moser had a license to make only 50,000 units per month. In a bid to expand his business, Puri decided that the best way to move forward was to export since the Indian government was quite supportive of exports.

As his business grew, the first of several technological changes in storage hit his company. Magnetic media starting giving way to optical media and CDs became the preferred storage media by the mid-1990s. Moser Baer set up its CD plant in 1998 with an investment of $78 million even when its own revenues were only $18 million.* Around 1998, Moser Baer's stock, which used to trade at ₹10 in 1995, bottomed at around ₹3. A perceptive investor who bought at ₹10 in 1995 with visions of a world full of computers would have been rewarded by 1998 with a significant erosion of his wealth. However, the investor who bought near the bottom perceiving CD-Rs as the future would be in for a better ride.

The bad news did not end with the CD-R plant. The vicious dynamics of the technology industry struck immediately. Within three months of the commissioning of the plant in 1999, the price of CD-Rs crashed from $7 to $1 when the manufacturing price was $1.5.** Moser Baer was losing 50 cents for every unit it sold. The stock did not do much over this period; it see-sawed between ₹4 and ₹8 between 1997 and 1999. Soon after starting optical media operations, Moser Baer, became the lowest cost producer of optical discs in the world and had the third largest capacity for making CD-Rs and DVDs.

Even though the company was facing huge losses on its CD sales, the macro picture was favourable for the company in that going forward it would turnout to be lucrative. The first batch of CDs were shipped primarily to play pre-recorded music, CDs had multimedia storage capability. On the sidelines, several developments took place that created huge market for the CDs. Sony's first version of CD Walkman — Discman D-50 was

---

* "Disc Driver", Anuradha Ranganathan, *Forbes Magazine,* 21 May 2007

** "Restless and Global", Deepak Puri, *Business Today,* Collectors' Issue, Volume 2, March 2005

launched in 1984. However the actual sales of portable CD players took off only in mid 1990s.

Microsoft launched its first version of CD ROM software Microsoft Bookshelf in 1987 to promote usage of CDs for data storage. Late 1980s and early 1990s saw increased usage of personal computers, which is evident from sales growth figures of computers. Between 1991 and 1997 sales of PCs grew from 18,750 to 81,000* (CAGR of 23.25%). The mid-1990s also saw evolution of the Internet, which produced millions of pieces of data daily that required a storage device that was reliable, could store huge volumes of data and had a long life and faster access. CDs scored over floppy discs exactly on these features. While a floppy disc's storage capacity was just 1.4 megabytes, a CD could store 650 megabytes of data. The life of CD — roughly 20 years — too was superior to that of the floppy disc.

All these factors translated into huge demand for CDs by 1998. When Moser Baer decided to start CD manufacturing, the global demand for recordable CDs was 1.10 billion units with annual growth rates of 250 %. For Moser Baer, which had plans to install a capacity of 150 million units, with production cost of just 40 cents per unit (*versus* global average of 70 cents), and a global selling price of $2 per disc, it was a profitable option.** Starting 1999, the technology boom in the US became recognized in India. Suddenly, computers were everywhere. This was the time when the NASDAQ market started making millionaires out of every college kid who could set up a webpage. Along with

---

* Data and stats compiled by Jeremy Reimer. Source: www.jeremyreimer.com/total_share.html

** Can Moser Baer Rewrite a Profitable Program?, Jaideep Lahiri, *Business Today*, 7 December 1999

all other things related to the IT industry, Moser Baer started rising. And what a rise it was. From a low of ₹3 in June 1997, Moser Baer went all the way up to a high of ₹190 in March 2000. If you had invested ₹10,000 in Moser Baer in June 1997, you would have had ₹6,00,000 by March 2000. Not a bad return by any measure. Following the tech bust in 2000, Moser Baer trended steadily down along with the rest of the market and bottomed out in November 2002 at ₹50 (*see* Figure VI.1).

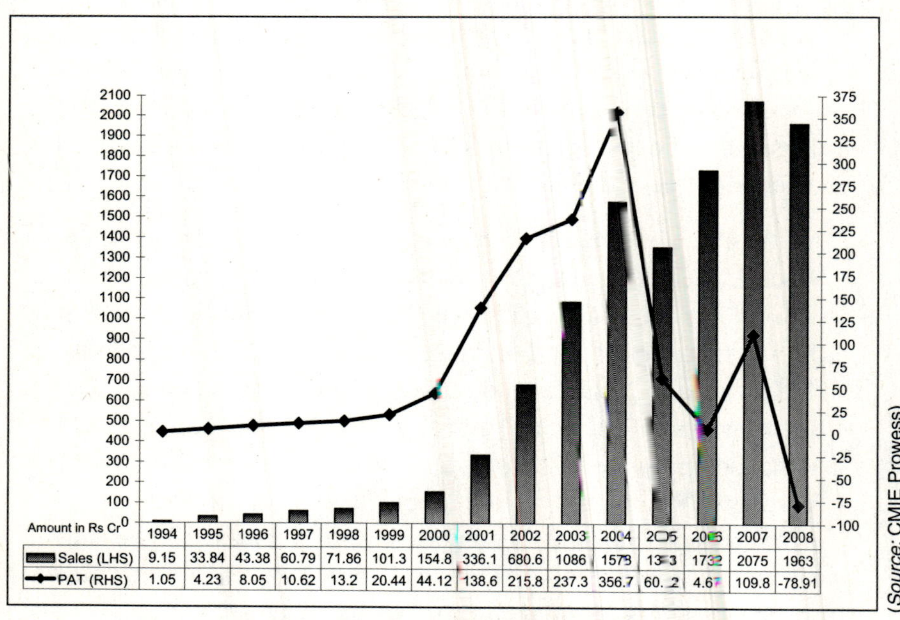

	1994	1995	1996	1997	1998	1999	2000	2001	2002	2003	2004	2005	2006	2007	2008
Sales (LHS)	9.15	33.84	43.38	60.79	71.86	101.3	154.8	336.1	680.6	1086	1578	13[illegible]3	1732	2075	1963
PAT (RHS)	1.05	4.23	8.05	10.62	13.2	20.44	44.12	138.6	215.8	237.3	356.7	60.[illegible]2	4.67	109.8	-78.91

Figure VI.1: **Sales and PAT of Moser Baer**

During this period, there was uncertainty regarding anti-dumping duties that the EU was considering imposing on foreign CD manufacturers, the technology bubble's burst had taken down everything related to technology. Moreover, there was another shift happening: video. The mass movement to DVDs in the home video market opened up a new opportunity for Moser Baer. In addition, in 2003 it won a long term outsourcing deal with Imation, a leading global producer of optical discs.

Again, a perceptive investor could have taken advantage of the bad sentiment towards technology to buy Moser Baer at an attractive price. If someone made the choice to buy the ₹50 bottom, by 2007, they would have multiplied their wealth 6 fold. The investor who bought the 1998 bottom would have made 100 times their original investment in 9 years.

Make no mistake: this stock was never easy to hold. The risk of technological obsolescence was always around the corner. If you thought the floppy disk market was attractive, CDs took over. If you bought it because CDs and DVDs looked like an interesting market, flash drives, larger hard disks, internet data centres, all posed threats. The only thing that could have kept you invested in the stock was faith in the management's capability. If you understood that they had successfully changed the business of the company several times in order to keep their company relevant, then you might have stayed invested. This is without talking about the intense volatility in the stock. If you were the type to get spooked by dramatic falls in price, you would not have captured this return. The stock went from ₹10 to ₹3 in 3 years, then went up to ₹190. From ₹190 it crashed to ₹50. Then again from ₹50, it rose to ₹330. From ₹330 it made a low of ₹140 during the sub-prime crisis (*see* Figure VI.2 and Table VI.1).

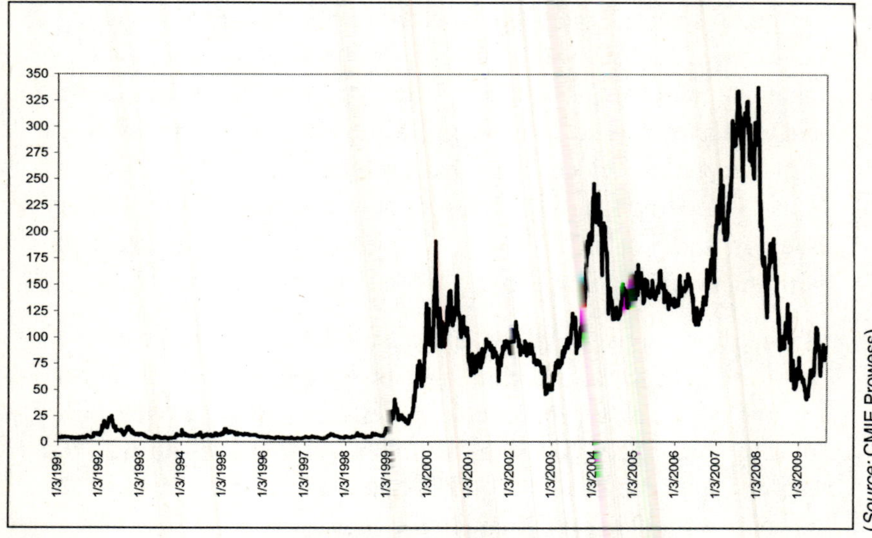

(*Source:* CMIE Prowess)

Figure VI.2: **The price chart of Moser Baer India Ltd**

Table VI.1

Growth in Moser Baer's P/E, Market Cap and Sales

	Starting (1995)	*Ending (2009)*	*CAGR*
P/E	22.73	-11.3	
Market Cap	35.92	1534.95	36.74
Sales	33.84	2076.8	40.92

(*Source:* CMIE Prowess)

Time-line

- 1983: Moser Baer established to make a variety of products.
- 1996: Expands manufacturing capacity of micro floppy diskettes to 93.6 million units per annum.
- 1997: Enters into a comprehensive agreement with three organization viz., Mag Media Ltd., IMTC and RES GmbH,

- 1998: Allots shares to IFC Washington at ₹12.01 per share.
- 1998: Floats subsidiaries in US and Germany.
- 1999: Sets up plant in Noida to manufacture CD-R and DVDs.
- 2000: Enters into R&D tie-up with 4M Technologies, leader in optical media.
- 2000: Acquires Capco and three leading European CDR brands.
- 2000: Enters audio media market through tie-up with Emtec Magnetics of Germany.
- 2000: Ties-up with Tips Industries in India to market BASF range of audio and video cassettes.
- 2003: Wins long term outsourcing deal from Imation.
- 2003: Starts marketing optical disks in its own brand.
- 2003: Ties-up with HP to launch Lightscribe optical media.
- 2006: Launches Moser Baer USB Flash drives.
- 2006: Enters into home entertainment.
- 2006: Enters into solar energy.
- 2008: Ties-up with Shemaroo Video to distribute international classics in India. Beefs up its distribution network of CDs and DVDs by distributing CDs and DVDs on cycle carts.

Example VII — Pantaloon Retail Ltd.

In 1999, Pantaloon was best known for a chain of franchise stores that sold garments. In 1997, it launched a large store in Kolkata that captured the imagination of customers and owned several garment brands such as Pantaloon, Bare, John Miller, Annabel and Shrishti. At the time, Pantaloon faced competition from established business houses such as Trent (Tatas) and Shoppers' Stop (Rahejas). It was not easy to predict that Pantaloon would be the retailing juggernaut that it had become by 2008. At that time it was said that Kishore Biyani aspired to be the Sam Walton of Indian retail. The investment community either indulged or derided this aspiration.

However, Biyani led the company from strength to strength over the next decade. He understood all the important aspects of retailing. As early as 2001, he had planned his real estate needs until 2008 and locked up the necessary properties. In addition, he understood the mind of the customer better than almost any other retailer in the country. Pantaloon also rapidly professionalized and hired some of the best available talent in the industry. The topline of the company grew from ₹91 crore in 1999 to ₹3,393 crore in 2007. However, in this period of manic expansion, the bottomline was not very consistent. This is a regular feature of companies that are expanding at such a breakneck pace.

The company had changed dramatically by 2008. Biyani had led Pantaloon to leadership of the Indian retail market, with presence in over 30 cities, big and small. The number of formats the company operated also increased dramatically. From simple supermarket formats to seamless malls offering everything from garments to food to electronics, the company covered the entire gamut. In addition, the company also started investing in other companies to increase its private label portfolio, started a real estate investment fund to buy properties for use by Pantaloon stores, and set up a private equity fund to invest in consumer-oriented companies. Kishore Biyani is now a poster child, not just for the success of Indian retail but also for Indian entrepreneurship.

Low Valuation

The organized retailing market at the time was very small in comparison to the total retail opportunity. Various studies at the time put the organized retail market at between 2% and 3% of the total retail market. A study by IRMC in 2005 put the Indian retail market at $300 billion. Even if we assume that in 1999, the market was less than a third of that, at $100 billion, i.e., ₹5,000 crore at that exchange rate, Pantaloon's market capitalization of ₹2.52 crore in 1999 was miniscule in comparison. If one looked at the financials of the company, Pantaloon's execution capabilities would have become very clear. Pantaloon grew sales at an astounding 80% clip per year, from ₹4.81 crore to ₹91.23 crore between 1993 and 1998. Profits also grew at a 50% growth rate per year to end up at ₹2.22 crore in 1998. In spite of this fantastic growth, Pantaloon was very poorly valued. In 1999, it traded at a P/E of 1.19. In spite of sales of over ₹90 crore, its market capitalization was ₹2.52 crore. Did one need any other measure of undervaluation? It provided a huge margin of safety. Even if the company's valuation became reasonable and ended at 1 times sales, you would see a stock price appreciation of nearly 40 times. This low valuation combined with the immense potential for organized retail offered a fantastic investment opportunity to those who were paying attention (*see* Figure VII.1).

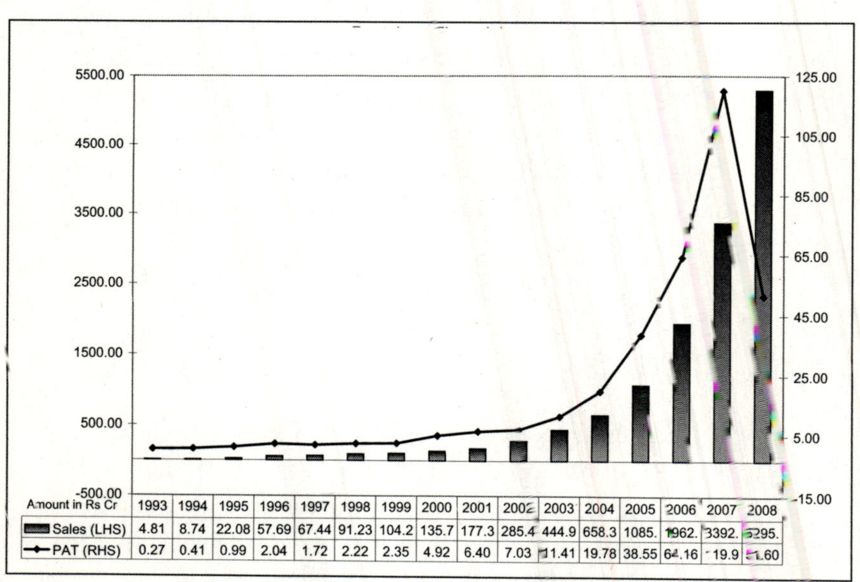

Amount in Rs Cr	1993	1994	1995	1996	1997	1998	1999	2000	2001	2002	2003	2004	2005	2006	2007	2008
Sales (LHS)	4.81	8.74	22.08	57.69	67.44	91.23	104.2	135.7	177.3	285.4	444.9	658.3	1085.	1962.	3392.	5295.
PAT (RHS)	0.27	0.41	0.99	2.04	1.72	2.22	2.35	4.92	6.40	7.03	11.41	19.78	38.55	64.16	119.9	51.60

(*Source:* CMIE Prowess)

Figure VII.1: **Sales and PAT of Pantaloon**

Volatility

The ride with Pantaloon has been nothing if not scary. From a low of ₹1.58 in 1999, the stock climbed to a high of ₹13 by January 2000. It rapidly lost 83% of its value by June 2000 and settled at ₹2.1. It rallied back equally rapidly to ₹5.86 in 2001, only to lose 50% of its value in 3 months time. From its September 2001 low of ₹2.5, the stock rallied to a high of ₹11.69 in May 2002. By August 2002, it had again slipped to ₹7.25, losing 38% of its value. From that low, the stock relentlessly rallied to ₹400 by April 2006. In the market collapse of May 2006, Pantaloon lost about 40% of its value to end up at ₹240. From this low, the stock rallied to a high of ₹830 by December 2007, only to lose 60% of its value by March 2008 (*see* Figure VII.2 and Table VII.1).

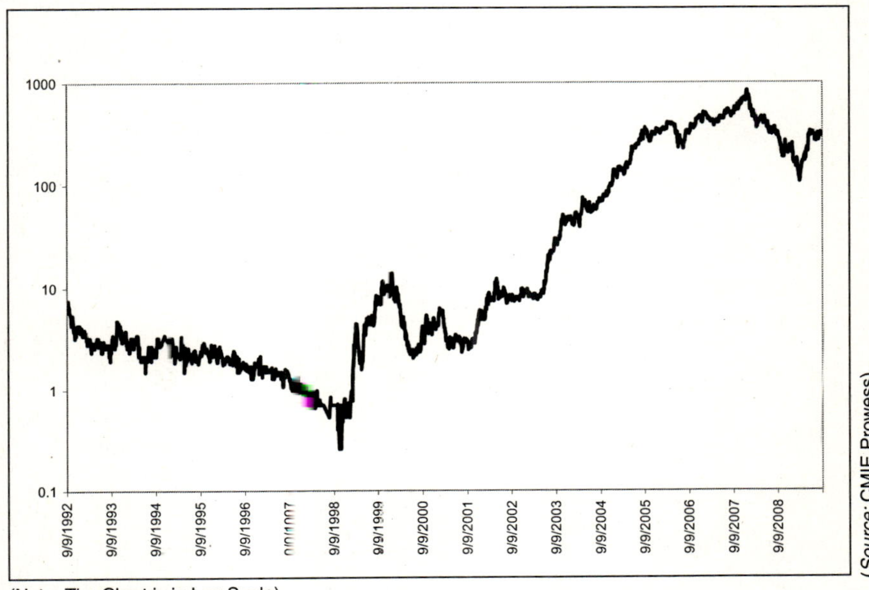

(Note: The Chart is in Log Scale)

Figure VII.2: **The price chart of Pantaloon Retail (India) Ltd**

Table VII.1

Growth in Pantaloon's P/E, Market Cap and Sales

	Starting (1992)	*Ending (2008)*	*CAGR*
P/E	54.16	43.51	
Market Cap (₹Cr)	13	5956.09	50.45%
Sales (₹Cr)	4.81	5295.88	59.51%

(*Source*: CMIE Prowess)

Exit

We don't believe it was time to exit this stock in 2008, given the enormous potential that the Indian market has for organized retailers.

Time-line

- 1987: Company incorporated as Manz Wear Pvt. Ltd. Launch of Pantaloons Trouser, India's first formal trouser brand.
- 1991: Launch of BARE, the Indian jeans brand
- 1992: IPO was made in the month of May.
- 1994: Company starts distribution of branded garments through franchise format retail outlet — The Pantaloon Shoppe.
- 1995: John Miller Brand launched.
- 2001: India's first hyper market chain, Big Bazaar, launched.
- 2004: Central mall launched in Bangalore
- 2005: Fashion Station chain — exclusive chain for plus-sized individuals launched.
- 2007: Future Capital Holdings — Company's financial arm launches real estate funds and its PE fund Kshitij with plans

to foray into insurance and consumer credit. Launches multiple retail formats including Collection I, Future Bazaar, Shoe Factory, E Zone, Home Depot and Futurebazaar.com

- 2008: Future Capital Holdings lists on NSE.

Example VIII — Unitech: The 1,400-bagger!

Owning a house was an unfulfilled dream for most Indians in post-independence India. Housing loans were too expensive and salaries were too low to support loan repayments. Only the top layer of society could afford to build or buy homes. But things began to change as liberalization finally took hold in the late 1990s.

Company Background

Unitech was established by Ramesh Chandra, a graduate of IIT-Kharagpur, in 1971 to carry on the business of turnkey construction of industrial and residential projects. Over the following decades, it built up a vast amount of experience in various kinds of industrial, residential, commercial and infrastructural projects. Pioneers of township development, the company launched its first such project near Lucknow in 1986. It also gained international experience by executing projects in far-flung places like Libya and

Kazakhstan. By the year 2003, they had become one of the most eminent developers in North India, with over 30 years of experience and a reputation for efficient execution of projects.

Unrecognized Change

In 1998, housing loans cost anywhere between 15% and 18%. By 2003, those same rates had fallen to between 8% and 10%. During the same period, HDFC's mortgage portfolio rose from ₹3,425 crore to ₹9,951 crore. Vijaya Bank grew its housing loan portfolio from ₹66 crore in 2001 to ₹482 crore in 2002. This period also coincided with spectacular salary increases of around 250% to 400% between 1997 and 2001.* Owning a house was an aspiration for most Indians and several of them were able to fulfil that dream as interest rates fell to multi-year lows in the 2002-2003 period. In 2002, the government also began to allow funds raised through external commercial borrowings to be used for investment in real estate. The stage was set for a huge real estate boom.

Low Market Capitalization

PSi Inc., an India-focused research firm headquartered in New York, estimates that 40% of global wealth is in real estate.** Assuming that India's 200 million middle class population had an average wealth of ₹1,00,000 each, the total size of this pool was about ₹20 lakh crore. If the PSi study is accurate, India's real estate market size was about ₹10 lakh crore. Unitech had a total market capitalization of ₹56 crore at the time. It was woefully undervalued.

---

* *Business Today,* 20 July 2003, "The Big H".

** *PSi Research,* September 2002, Real Estate Industry in India.

Performance

Investors who purchased Unitech any time between 1995 and 2002 would have achieved a return of nearly 1,400 times their original investment by December 2007. Between 1995 and 2002, it would have been very frustrating to hold it though because the stock went down 30% in this period at several points. Moreover, the Asian crisis that hit in 1997 and ravaged the real estate market and would have made any investor extremely nervous. However, if the entry were made in 2002, things were much more sanguine. Global interest rates were extremely low and a benign environment was created for real estate. Most investors would have been alerted to this opportunity in 2002 rather than in 1995.

The greater challenge for investors in Unitech would have been to bet on change rather than on demonstrated improvement in sales or profits. Unitech's sales grew at an annual rate of roughly 12% between 1990 and 2002. Its profits grew at an even slower rate of 4%. However, as some recompense, the valuation of Unitech was quite undemanding with a P/E of 3 in 2002. An investor in Unitech would necessarily have had to keep faith in the real estate story in order to stay invested. In fact, most investors who were sensitive to the real estate opportunity in 2002 would have looked at Unitech's anaemic financial performance and backed off from it. But what a ride they would have missed! As the real estate boom progressed in India, Unitech's performance improved dramatically. Between 2002 and 2007 its sales grew at an impressive rate of 50% and profits at an even faster clip of 128%. But unless one bought into the real estate story in 2002 or 2003, it would have been very difficult to capture the dramatic rise in the Unitech stock.

Exit

By 2007, perhaps there were enough reasons to consider exiting Unitech. The Indian real estate market had become highly speculative. Unitech had become an institutional stock. Several institutions that did not buy it early on, now plunged in. Unitech's market cap rose from ₹57 crore in 2007 to ₹79,260 crore in 2007. In addition to real estate becoming speculative, the Indian rupee had appreciated significantly since 2006, putting pressure on the margins of IT companies. This would eventually have resulted in a squeeze on the liberal pay raises that IT companies would give to their employees. Moreover, the Reserve Bank of India, in an attempt to control inflation kept interest rates high even though the economy was visibly weakening. High interest rates combined with lowered expectations of salary would, inevitably, result in a cool-off in the housing market. It was also becoming obvious that the housing market was extremely overbuilt, at least in the short run. Another phenomenon to watch was that new real estate companies were listing on the stock exchange almost every week. It became very difficult to differentiate between one and the other by late 2007.

None of this is to suggest that Unitech could not go up higher. In fact, in my opinion, it was still possible for Unitech to deliver reasonable returns going forward (*see* Table VIII.1 and Figures VIII.1 and VIII.2).

Table VIII.1

Growth in Unitech's P/E, Market Cap and Sales

	Starting (2003)	*Ending (2009)*	*CAGR*
P/E	8.15	46.64	
Market Cap (₹cr)	56.07	27089	141.79%
Sales (₹cr)	212.90	1845.08	20%

(*Source:* CMIE Prowess)

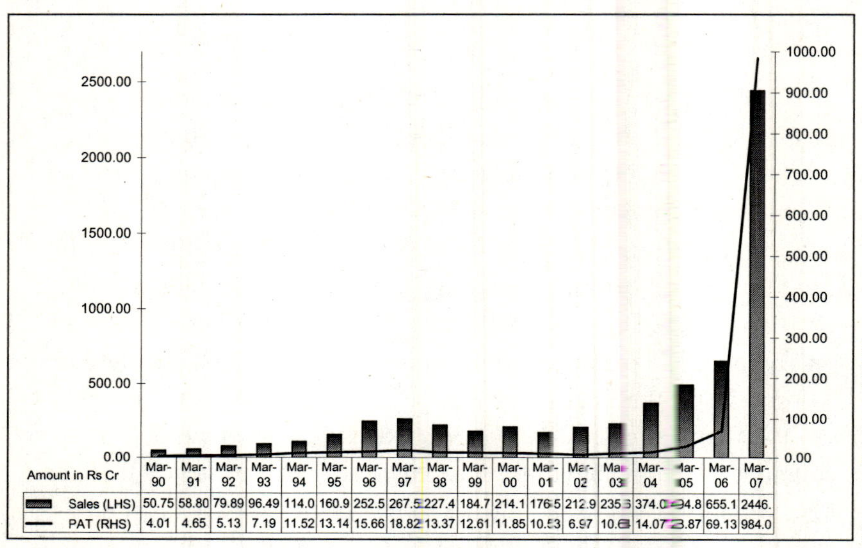

Amount in Rs Cr	Mar-90	Mar-91	Mar-92	Mar-93	Mar-94	Mar-95	Mar-96	Mar-97	Mar-98	Mar-99	Mar-00	Mar-01	Mar-02	Mar-03	Mar-04	Mar-05	Mar-06	Mar-07
Sales (LHS)	50.75	58.80	79.89	96.49	114.0	160.9	252.5	267.5	227.4	184.7	214.1	176.5	212.9	[illegible]	374.0	[illegible]	655.1	2446.
PAT (RHS)	4.01	4.65	5.13	7.19	11.52	13.14	15.66	18.82	13.37	12.61	11.85	10.53	6.97	[illegible]	14.07	[illegible]	69.13	984.0

Figure VIII.1: **Sales and PAT of Unitech**

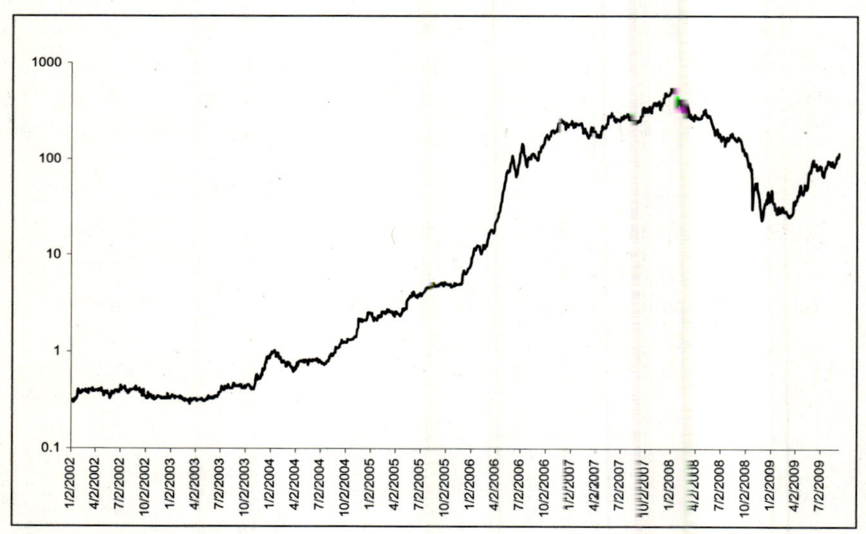

(Note: This chart is in log scale)

Figure VIII.2: **The price chart of Unitech Ltd**

Time-Line

- 1987: Receives major orders from Vizag Steel Plant.
- 1992: Announces a rights issue in the ratio of 1:2.
- 1994: Enters MOU with Singapore Consortium and Haryana Urban Development Authority for setting up Technology Park in Gurgaon.
- 1995: Enters into partnership with Resources Development Corporation Ltd., Singapore and Comcraft Asia Pacific Pte Ltd.
- 2005: Becomes the largest listed real estate company in India, with a turnover of ₹500 crore.
- 2006: Announces bonus issue in the ratio of 12: 1.

  Enters agreement with IST Ltd. for development of Software / IT Park.
- 2007: Announces bonus issue in the ratio of 1:1.

Example IX — United Spirits Ltd.

Vijay Mallya definitely does not fit the textbook mould of a CEO. His flamboyance combined with the lackluster profits generated by his flagship companies, United Breweries (UB) and United Spirits, make it very difficult for an investor to make a decision to buy his companies. I personally was never able to buy either one of his companies because I was flummoxed by the very large sales and miniscule profits they produced in businesses which I thought should be cash cows. My mistrust of Mr. Mallya cost me a fortune in lost opportunity. The stock went from ₹31 in 2001 to ₹2,000 in December 2007, a gain of nearly 64 times. I am now much wiser — and much poorer!

United Spirits owns some of the largest brands in the Indian liquor market. In 2001, it owned McDowell's, one of the most popular whiskey brands in the country with several sub-brands under it. United Spirits was originally just McDowell & Co. It was acquired by Vijay Mallya's father, Vittal Mallya. In 1972-73, the elder Mallya also acquired Herbertson's from the Anglo-Thai Corporation. Under Vittal Mallya's leadership, Herbertson's launched Romanov Vodka, Bagpiper Whiskey, High Society Gin and Royal Treasure Rum in the 1970s. In the 1980s,

Vijay Mallya built McDowell's brands such as No.1 Whiskey, No.1 Brandy and Diplomat Whiskey. Both Herbertson and McDowell aggressively built their brands through the 1980s and 1990s, using all forms of media available at the time. Unlike other liquor producers of the time, such as Mohan Meakins or Khoday, Vijay Mallya hired professional management and delegated responsibility to them. This agglomeration of liquor businesses was then collectively referred to as United Breweries' spirits division. By 2001-2002, UB's spirits division was ranked fifth in global unit volume by Impact International, a New York based research firm. UB's spirits division had total sales of 26 million units, just behind Bacardi. In March 2005, McDowell's acquired Shaw Wallace & Co., becoming the second largest liquor maker in the world.

Low Valuation

In 2001, the Indian stock market was in the doldrums. Even though UB's spirits division had 26 mllion units in sales and was considered the fifth largest seller of liquor by volume in the world, it had a market capitalization of only ₹159 crore. Sales at the time were ₹1,134 crore. Unbelievably, the world's fifth largest seller of alcoholic beverages, was selling at a price of 14% of its sales! At the time, UB's liquor division was supposed to have a market share of 35%.* So the total market at the time was estimated to be roughly ₹3,500 crore. McDowell's market capitalization was less than 5% of industry size. Even if there were no growth in the industry, this would have been considered undervalued.

---

* *The Hindu Business Line,* 12 December 2002.

Financial Performance

Though sales growth was quite good, profits had always been a challenge for the company. When asked about this situation in 1995, Vijay Mallya replied:

> "Because of price control and highly regulated distribution and marketing policies, the profits remain low." Some might have blamed big and perhaps unnecessary expenses such as his personal jet.* Whatever the reason, a much smaller player, Radico Khaitan, had a better profitability track record than Mallya's companies. However, Mallya's ambitious growth plans ensured that sales continued to grow very rapidly and the stock price more than kept up.

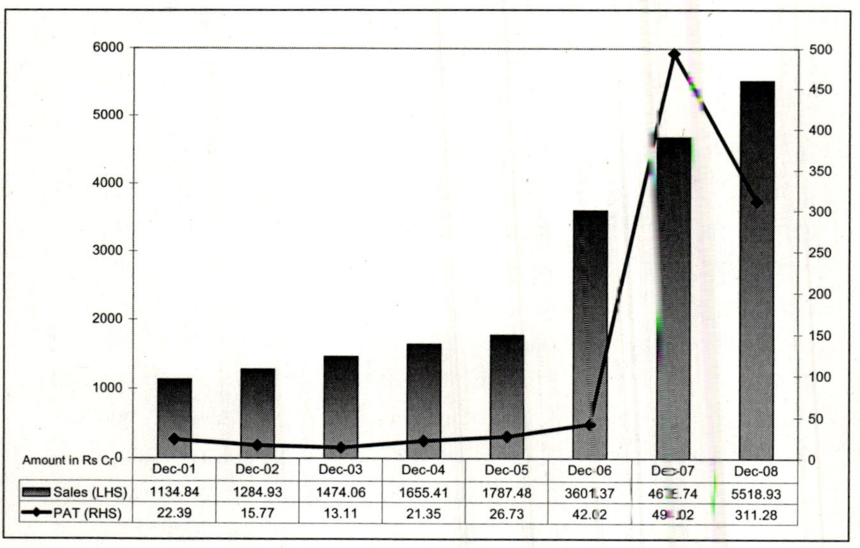

	Dec-01	Dec-02	Dec-03	Dec-04	Dec-05	Dec-06	Dec-07	Dec-08
Sales (LHS)	1134.84	1284.93	1474.06	1655.41	1787.48	3601.37	467[illegible].74	5518.93
PAT (RHS)	22.39	15.77	13.11	21.35	26.73	42.02	49[illegible].02	311.28

Figure IX.1: **Sales and PAT of United Spirits Ltd**

---

* *Business Today*, 10 April 2005. All Work and No Play?

Volatility

From a low of ₹31 in 2001, the stock, then called McDowell & Co., rallied very quickly to ₹70. But it began a slow and systematic decline all the way back to ₹33 by 2003. It rallied back up to ₹73 in December 2003 but crashed back to ₹45 by June 2004. It was around this time that rumours of the Shaw Wallace buy began circulating. The stock began a relentless rally from ₹48 in July 2004 to make a high of ₹870 in March 2006. But in the May 2006 market meltdown, it lost about 50% of its value to settle down at ₹400. In the recovery that followed, the stock went all the way up to ₹2,000 in December 2008. The ride, while exhilarating, was definitely not easy. The volatility in this stock, again, shows the power of holding on to a good story rather than obsessively trading it (*see* Figure IX.2 and Table IX.1).

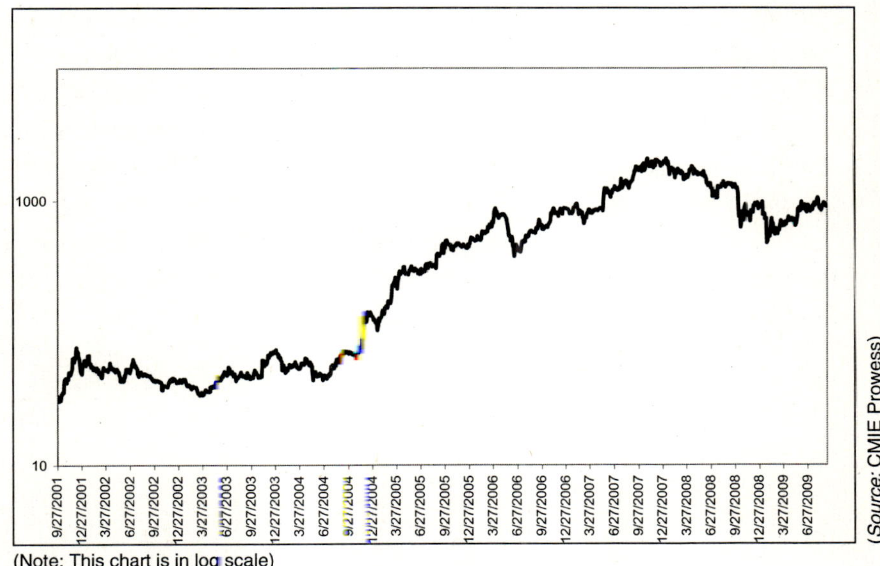

(*Source:* CMIE Prowess)

(Note: This chart is in log scale)

Figure IX.2: **The price chart of United Spirits Ltd**

Table IX.1

Growth in United Spirits P/E, Market Cap and Sales

	Starting (2001)	*Ending (2009)*	*CAGR*
P/E	7.77	33.83	
Market Cap (₹Cr)	159.81	9732.08	98.35%
Sales (₹Cr)	1134.37	5513.93	30.17%

(Note: Sales are for the financial year 2008) *(Source: Prowess, CMIE)*

Exit

In 2008, United Spirits was definitely not an exit. First, it was the second largest liquor company in the world. Domestically, its brands are well established and promotion of liquor brands is prohibited in India. Even if foreign brands enter India, it would be really tough for them to beat United Spirits and build their brands and set up a nation wide distribution network, given the complexities involved. Most importantly, liquor industry is under regulatory control, be it retail distribution or the tax structure. For instance, various taxes constitute 62% of MRP. In such a tough environment, only companies with killer brands in their portfolio and a nationwide presence can survive. Culturally, the attitude towards alcohol consumption is fast changing. United Spirits also announced entry into wines business and was scouting for reputed global brands to have a global footprint.

Example X — Zee Entertainment

In 1991, Saddam Hussein unwittingly created a revolution in India. Until then, the only TV channel available to Indian viewers was Doordarshan. Like most other state run channels around the world, Doordarshan tended to be monotonous and lacked entertainment content. The goal of the government was not to entertain but to provide educational and informational content. Most Indians found entertainment at the cinema. TV had yet to turn into the entertainment source of choice for the entire family. However, the first Gulf War in 1991 changed all that.

Indians who had never heard of satellite TV or CNN suddenly were exposed to live blow-by-blow coverage of the war. Doordarshan was beaming CNN clips into Indian living rooms during the 1991 Gulf War. Soon after that, Richard Li, based in Hong Kong, launched Star TV, offering five channels *via* satellite across Asia. Very soon, enterprising cable operators sprung up in every neighbourhood. Using very rudimentary coaxial cable strung over bamboo poles, they soon started providing India's entertainment-hungry audience with content provided *via* satellite from Hong Kong. However, local content was still not available.

In 1992, Subhash Chandra, a former grain trader from Hissar, Haryana, identified this opportunity. Chandra launched Zee TV, India's first Hindi language satellite channel, freeing Indians from the monotony of Doordarshan. Suddenly, content available to Indian viewers changed from farm-education programs to family dramas, cartoons, talk shows, cookery shows and soap operas. The Indian audience lapped this up enthusiastically. The media industry's size expanded as more and more people started watching TV. In 1992, it was estimated to be ₹1,200 crore. By 1999 it had grown to ₹10,000 crore (*see* Figure IX.1).*

Soon, other players including Sony, Star, ETV in the Andhra Pradesh, Sun TV in Tamil Nadu and several others entered the fray. In the meanwhile, Zee's relationship with Star began to unravel. Since 1992, Zee had been up linking four of its channels through Star's AsiaSAT on a lease bases. In August 1999, Zee decided to break away from its relationship with Star and moved its allegiance to Turner International (India) Ltd. As part of its break-up with Star, it had to purchase Star's stake in Asia Today Ltd., which was a 50-50 JV between Zee and Star. Zee paid Star $150 million for its 50 per cent stake and agreed to waive the non-compete agreement that Zee and Star had entered into.

If one looked at Zee during early 1990s when it was the only listed company in that space, it offered a good investment proposition. The company was changing rapidly. It was trying to grab every opportunity on its way. It first started as a television content provider to the Zee TV channel. And in 1994, within two years, it promoted Siticable to provide cable network facility to local cable operators on a city-by-city basis. This was an attempt to capture cable distribution network. The same year it

* Alakumar Subramanian, "Sify Finance", *The Media Mogul and his Empire'*, 03 August 2003

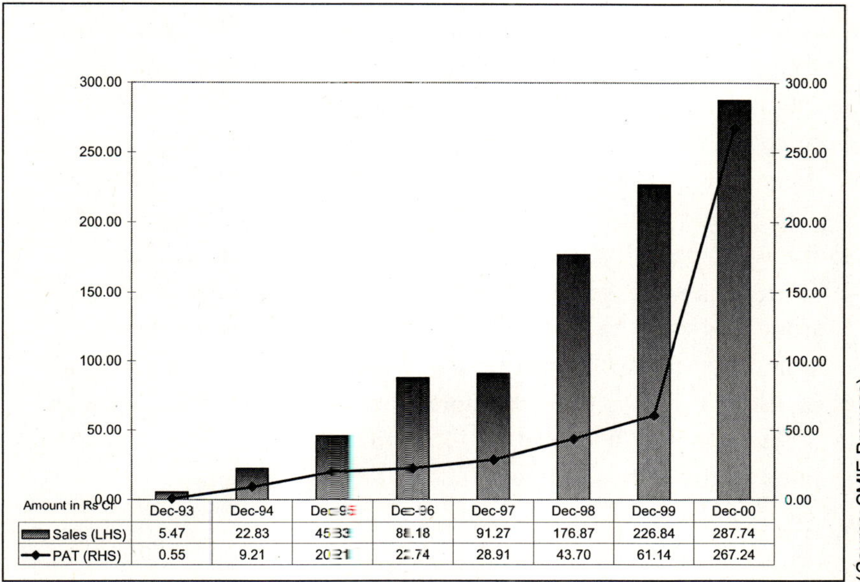

	Dec-93	Dec-94	Dec-95	Dec-96	Dec-97	Dec-98	Dec-99	Dec-00
Sales (LHS)	5.47	22.83	45.33	88.18	91.27	176.87	226.84	287.74
PAT (RHS)	0.55	9.21	20.21	22.74	28.91	43.70	61.14	267.24

Figure X.1: **Sales and PAT of Zee Entertainment**

---

introduced the concept of paid channels in India by launching a 24-hour channel, Zee Cinema, a channel dedicated to Hindi films and film-related programming. The channel was a success. In the same year, Zee forged an alliance with News Corp to use its global distribution network to target Indian residing in Hong Kong. In 1997 it launched Zee Cine awards which, unlike other film awards in India, were based on public opinion — a first of its kind in India — and was received well by the audience. To synergize the content it developed for Zee Cinema, it also ventured into publications by launching *Zee Premier Magazine.* The magazine was a flop as it could not withstand the competition from magazines like Filmfare.

Interestingly, while all these developments were taking place, the Zee stock did nothing. The market did not recognize this change.

It was this unrecognized change that provided the opportunity for perceptive investors. Zee's stock price languished around ₹10 (adjusted for splits and bonuses) between 1993 and 1998. At this price, the market cap was ₹141 crore. During this phase, the media sector was growing and Zee was taking up many initiatives. The patient investor would have been really frustrated in this five-year period. Even though the company was making great strides, its stock price did not move. The company' sales went from ₹5.4 crore in 1993 to ₹91 crore in 1997. Profits ballooned from ₹50 lakh to ₹29 crore in 1997. However, the market was inclined to ignore this. Investors who bought the stock between 1993 and 1997, and held on to it until 2000 would have multiplied their wealth 150 times.

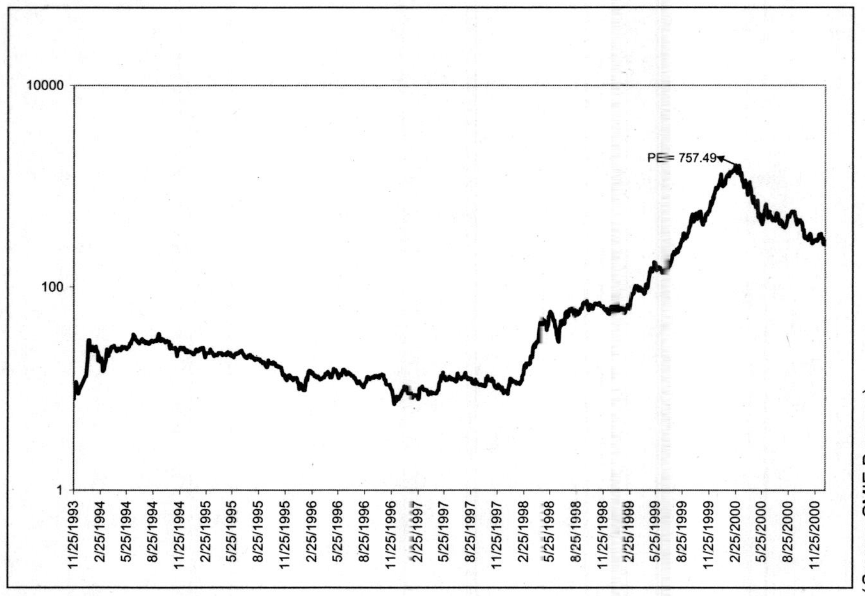

(Note: This Chart is in log scale)

Figure X.2: **The price chart of Zee Entertainment Enterprises Ltd**

Table X.1

Growth in Zee Entertainment's P/E, Market Cap and Sales

	Starting (1993)	*Ending (2000)*	*CAGR*
P/E	59.75	757.49	
Market Cap (₹Cr)	49.38	60.394.66	82%
Sales (₹Cr)	5.4	287.17	48.79%

(*Source:* CMIE Prowess)

It has to be mentioned at this point that Zee Telefilms was one of the infamous K-10 stocks. The stock price, which hit, ₹1,555.05 at the height of the 2000 boom did not see that level again. In fact, in just 1999 itself the stock went up 10-fold, However, our belief is that the reason Zee was one of the K-10 stocks was because of its phenomenal growth and opportunity. A stock boom or the manipulation of a certain stock typically happens only because there is a grain of truth in it to begin with.

Exit Call

A combination of factors would have triggered an exit call in the stock in 1999. The first was a meteoric rise of the stock price — the stock gave a return of 10x in just one year. Most importantly, its market cap was double the size of market opportunity. While the market for satellite channels was estimated at ₹10,000 crore in 1999, by October 1999, the market cap of Zee was ₹17,364 cr.

There are several lessons to be learnt from Zee:

- Lack of market recognition can persist for several years.
- Most of the gains from a stock can come in a very short period of time.
- A vertical rise combined with a high valuation (757 P/E) when there are real earnings usually indicates a top.

- When market capitalization nearly equals industry size, it is probably a top.

Time-line

- 1991: Gulf War, CNN takes off in India.
- 1991: Star TV launch.
- 1992: Zee TV launch — India's first private Hindi channel.
- 1994: Siticable launch.
- 1994: First 24-hr Hindi movie channel, Zee Cinema, launched as a paid channel.
- 1994: Forges alliance with Rupert Murdoch's News Corp.
- 1997: Launches India's first public opinion-based film awards, Zee Cine Awards.
- 1998: Zee broadcasted in the US through EchoStar's DTH platform.
- 1999: Launch of Alpha regional language bouquet and 3 English channels.
- 1999: Zee / Star TV end collaboration and break non-compete.
- 1999: Ties up with French company Canal Plus as a precursor to the launch of DTH service in India.

Index